THE IRISH-AMERICANS

THE IRISH-AMERICANS

BEFORE THE MOLLY MAGUIRES

The Emergence of the Ethno-Religious Factor in the Politics of the Lower Anthracite Region, 1844-1872

William A. Gudelunas, Jr.
and
William G. Shade

ARNO PRESS

A New York Times Company

New York — 1976

Editorial Supervision: ANDREA HICKS

———◆———

First publication in book form, 1976,
  by Arno Press, Inc.
Copyright © 1976 by William A. Gudelunas, Jr.

THE IRISH-AMERICANS
ISBN for complete set: 0-405-09317-9
See last pages of this volume for titles.

Manufactured in the United States of America

———◆———

Library of Congress Cataloging in Publication Data

Gudelunas, William A
    Before the Molly Maguires.

    (The Irish-Americans)
    Originally presented as the authors' thesis,
Lehigh University, 1973.
    Bibliography: p.
    1. Schuylkill Co., Pa.--Politics and government.
I. Shade, William G., joint author. II. Title.
III. Series.
F157.S3G82 1976   301.5'92'0974817 76-6344
ISBN 0-405-09339-X

Before the Molly Maguires: the Emergence of the Ethno-Religious

Factor in the Politics of the Lower Anthracite Region, 1844-1872

by

William A. Gudelunas, Jr.

and

William G. Shade

Preface

Much of the data and the general interpretation presented here
appeared in a much different form in Professor Gudelunas' 1972 Lehigh
University doctoral dissertation. Since that time the authors have
done a good deal of further research and have applied more sophistocated
analytical methods to the data intending to publish as articles and
part of a larger work on political development in the mid-nineteenth
century. We are extremely happy that Arno Press asked us to put the
material we had collected together in the form of this book. We would
like to thank Elizabeth MacAdam, Theresa Racosky, and especially Mary
Lou Shade for helping us with our pleasant task.

W. A. G.
W. G. S.

Table of Contents

Introduction: Parties and the People
in Nineteenth Century America

The anthracite region of Pennsylvania has long been known
as the scene of intense social conflict. Class antagonism was more
pronounced in the coal districts than in any other industrial area
in the mid-nineteenth century United States. Mining entrepreneurs
achieved fortunes comparable to the great railroad and oil magnates
of the period, while mine laborers were among the most exploited workers in the country.[1] Unionization, which was fervently resisted by
anthracite corporations, failed to rectify these abuses during the
nineteenth century.[2]

The most spectacular result of this exploitation of labor in
the mining areas was the rise of the famous Molly Maguire associations.[3]
Most historians have perceived the ultimate goal of the Mollies as
the betterment of the conditions of anthracite laborers in general, and
have excused their lapses into rascist arguments on economic grounds.
The Irish did fear that operators would eventually import Black labor
to further undermine their working conditions in the anthracite area.[4]
Hence, the Mollies have represented the aspirations of poor white workers who opposed the privileged mining entrepreneurs. The Molly Maguires

---

[1] Wayne C. Broehl, Jr., The Molly Maguires (Cambridge, 1965),
and also Clifton K. Yearley, Enterprise and Anthracite: Economics and
Democracy in Schuylkill County, 1820-1875 (Baltimore, 1961) detail the
deplorable condition of miners in the anthracite region.

[2] Yearley, Enterprise and Anthracite, pp. 181-183.

[3] In Enterprise and Anthracite Yearley viewed the Mollies as
an organization which was in reality a labor union forced underground
by corporate attacks upon overt unionism.

[4] Broehl, The Molly Maguires, p. 87.

were a manifestation of the frustrations suffered by the poor of the anthracite region.[5]

This situation has led most historians to interpret the political behavior in the anthracite region in terms of this economic conflict; the rich and poor polarized politically just as they had economically and socially. It was the age-old story of the "haves" opposing the "have-nots." One party attracted the laborers and the other concentrated its strength among the business classes.

Traditional historical studies dealing with the socio-economic composition of political parties in the mid-nineteenth century United States have assumed that economic conflict was the basis of American political behavior.[6] Regarding the voter as an essentially rational, "economic man," selecting his partisan affiliation on the basis of the interests of his own specific economic group, the Progressive historians depicted the Democrats as the party of the poor working men and the unprivileged farmers.[7] Conversely, the Whigs and their successors, the

---

[5] The studies of the Molly Maguires are quite numerous. The most important include along with Broehl's book: Anthony J. Bimba, The Molly Maguires (New York, 1932); Walter J. Coleman, The Molly Maguire Riots: Industrial Conflict in the Pennsylvania Coal Region (New York, 1936); and Arthur H. Lewis, Lament for the Molly Maguires (New York, 1969).

[6] Two famous works which emphasize class differences between the political parties are: Charles A. Beard and Mary R. Beard, The Rise of American Civilization (New York, 1927); and Wilfred A. Binkley, American Political Parties, Their Natural History (New York, 1943).

[7] See Richard Hofstadter, The Progressive Historians (New York, 1968), for the best general discussion of this group.

Republicans, represented the privileged few and non-productive, speculative enterprise which existed at the expense of the toiling masses who actually produced our nation's wealth. In brief, class conflict underlay partisan behavior and politically polarized the rich and poor; the "real" issues which separated the parties were economic ones.[8]

In their discussion of the Civil War era, the Progressive historians pictured the Republicans as the party which appealed basically to the business interests of the North.[9] While they rhetorically supported many idealistic programs, these scholars argued that in fact the Republicans used these to conceal the true class basis upon which their activities were predicated. For example, the "clap trap" over the freedmen's civil rights disguised their true goal: the passage of legislation which would enhance the position of the American industrial community.[10] Economic cleavages were in essence responsible for political behavior among the voters in the United States.

---

[8] Arthur M. Schlesinger, Jr., The Age of Jackson (Boston, 1945), makes the classic statement of this position. He relies heavily on, Dixon Ryan Fox, The Decline of the Aristocracy in the Politics of New York, 1801-1840 (New York, 1919).

[9] Reinhard Luthin, The First Lincoln Campaign (Cambridge, 1944), Howard K. Beale, "The Tariff and Reconstruction", American Historical Review, XXXV (January, 1930), pp. 276-294; Beale, The Critical Year: A Study of Andrew Johnson and Reconstruction (New York, 1930); William B. Hesseltine, Lincoln and the War Governors (New York, 1955); Hesseltine, "Economic Factors in the Abandonment of Reconstruction," Mississippi Valley Historical Review, XXII (September, 1935), pp. 191-210; and C. Vann Woodward, Reunion and Reaction: The Compromise of 1877 and the End of Reconstruction (Boston, 1951).

[10] This theme is generally associated with the works of Howard K. Beale cited in the previous footnote.

Modifications of the Progressive interpretation of nineteenth century political behavior have emerged since World War II. A number of historians, for example, challenged the view popularized by Arthur M. Schlesinger, Jr., that laborers generally supported the party of Jackson in the ante-bellum period. These revisionists have shown that Jackson and his party were unsympathetic to America's early labor movement and that the poorest wards of America's cities in this period were by no means inevitably Jacksonian.[11] At the same time a related group of Schlesinger's critics argued that the Democrats of the 1830's and 1840's represented the rising or "expectant" capitalists while the Whigs attracted men from the older, more entrenched monied circles.[12] This "entreprenurial" interpretation of American politics rested upon a belief that leaders of both parties accepted a liberal-capitalist consensus on the nature of the American economy and political differences constituted conflicts between special interest groups. These historians, while rejecting the Progressives' economic interpretation, continued to view economic interest as the basis of political behavior.

------

[11] Richard B. Morris, "Andrew Jackson Strikebreaker," American Historical Review, LV (October, 1949), pp. 54-68; William A. Sullivan, "Did Labor Support Andrew Jackson?", Political Science Quarterly, (June, 1949), pp. 568-580; Edward Pessen, "Did Labor Support Andrew Jackson?: The Boston Story," Political Science Quarterly, LXIV (June, 1949), pp. 264-274; and Walter Hugins, Jacksonian Democracy and the Working Class (Stanford, 1960).

[12] Richard Hofstadter, The American Political Tradition and the Men Who Made It (New York, 1948); Bray Hammond, Banks and Politics in America from the Revolution to the Civil War (Princeton, 1957); Stanley Cohen, "Northeastern Business and Radical Reconstruction: A Re-Examination", Mississippi Valley Historical Review, LXVI (June, 1959), pp. 67-90, and Robert Sharkey, Money, Class, and Party: An Economic Study of the Civil War and Reconstruction (Baltimore, 1959).

The Progressives' economic interpretation of nineteenth century
American political behavior has also been challenged from another per-
spective by historians who have denied the importance of social conflict
in American state politics before the Civil War.[13] These historians
argued that there were few clearly definable differences in the economic
makeup of the parties' constituencies and insisted that political conflict be viewed in relation to the quest for power on the part of political
leaders seeking personal advancement.[14] Parties were, therefore, similar
in their social makeup and bestunderstood as electoral machines reflect-
ing the desires of powerful leaders.

Each of these interpretations of American political behavior
has been challenged in turn by historians who have emphasized the importance ethno-religious factors in determining political allegiance. The
most important advocate of this view is Lee Benson who analysed Jacksonian
politics in New York State.[15] Benson, arguing that economic interpretations
were too simple, believed that human response to political stimuli

---

[13] The foremost historian of this school was Roy F. Nichols.
For examples of his work see: The Democratic Machine, 1850-1854 (New
York, 1923); The Disruption of the American Democracy (New York, 1948);
The Stakes of Power (New York, 1961), and The Invention of the American
Political Parties (New York, 1967).

[14] The most important work from the Nichols' "school" has been
that of Richard McCormack: "Suffrage Classes and Party Alignment: A
Study in Voter Behavior," Mississippi Valley Historical Review, XLVI
(December, 1959), pp. 397-410; "New Perspectives on Jacksonian Politics,"
American Historical Review, (January, 1960), pp. 288-301; and The Second
American Party System: Party Formation in the Jacksonian Era (Chapel
Hill, 1966).

[15] Lee Benson, The Concept of Jacksonian Democracy: New York
as a Test Case (Princeton, 1961).

reflected the effects of not one, but a combination of variables effect-
ing the individual voter in many different ways.[16] A person's voting
behavior would often be determined by a "negative" or "positive" reference
to cultural symbolism associated with a specific group or person.[17]
Generally, Benson concluded that the voters of New York State identified
most directly with ethno-religious groups; hence, ethno-religious factors
were the primary determinants of voting behavior during the Jacksonian
period in the state of New York.

Several recent writers have joined Benson in acclaiming the
potency of ethno-religious factors in determining mid-nineteenth century
voting patterns.[18] These historians, who have focused on the analysis of
voting behavior in selected local areas, have indicated the importance of
these factors in Northern politics throughout the entire nineteenth century.
Most of these areas were affected by the same tensions which also influenced the anthracite region of which Schuylkill County was a part.

Each of these various interpretations has affected historians'
views of political behavior in Pennsylvania in the mid-nineteenth century.

---

[16] Benson discusses his theory of voting behavior at length
in The Concept of Jacksonian Democracy, pp. 270-287.

[17] Ibid., p. 281. See: Gene Wise, "Political 'Reality' in
Recent American Scholarship: Progressives versus Symbolists," American
Quarterly, XIX (Summer, 1967), pp. 303-328.

[18] Richard Jensen, "The Religious and Occupational Roots of
Party Identification: Illinois and Indiana in the 1870's," Civil War
History XVL (December, 1970), pp. 325-343; Paul Kleppner, The Cross
of Culture: A Social Analysis of Midwestern Politics, 1850-1900
(New York, 1970); Ronald P. Formisano, The Birth of Mass Political
Parties: Michigan, 1827-1861 (Princeton, 1971); and Roger Wyman,
"Wisconsin Ethnic Groups and the Election of 1890," Wisconsin Magazine
of History, LI (Summer, 1968), pp. 269-93.

For example, economic arguments were directly defended in many of the
early works which considered the Whigs of the 1830's and 1840's the
high tariff party of the Keystone State. The high tariff Whigs were
the party of the better classes while the Democrats represented the low
tariff proclivities of the poorer groups in Pennsylvania. In the 1850's
the widespread desire for tariff protection led Pennsylvanians to support
the Republicans and was ultimately responsible for Lincoln's nomination
and for later Radical policy.[19]

One of the critics of Schlesinger's views concerning labor
and Jacksonian Democracy also focused on the Keystone State. In a
series of articles which eventually appeared as a book, William Sullivan
found no strong link between common laborers and the party of Jackson
in Philadelphia and several other cities.[20] This work challenged arguments which described clearly defined economic political divisions which
pitted capital against labor.

Several other writers, influenced by Roy Nichols and concerned
primarily with Pennsylvania politics, accepted the importance of economic

[19] Henry Mueller, The Whig Party in Pennsylvania (New York,
1922); Reinhard Luthin, "Pennsylvania and Lincoln's Rise to the
Presidency," Pennsylvania Magazine of History and Biography, LXVII
(January, 1943), pp. 61-82; Richard Current, Old Thad Stevens: A
Story of Ambition (Madison, 1942); Ira Brown, "William D. Kelley and
Radical Reconstruction", Pennsylvania Magazine of History and Biography,
LXXXV (January, 1961), pp. 316-329.

[20] William Sullivan, The Industrial Worker in Pennsylvania,
1800-1840 (Harrisburg, 1955).

interests, but generally concerned themselves with the political machines
and leading politicians.[21] Far more aware than their predecessors of the
web of social pressures and the variety of group allegiances influencing
the voter, these historians turned to the machinations of politicians to
explain political behavior in nineteenth century Pennsylvania.

Recently historians directly or indirectly influenced by Lee
Benson have already applied the outlines of an ethno-religious interpretation of voting behavior to Pennsylvania. These studies generally
deny the primacy of purely economic factors and avoid even the moderate
adherence to the economic interpretation associated with the Nichols
school. Instead they focus upon social and cultural responses to economic
and demographic change.[22] Not only the effect of the tariff and bank
issues, but even that of other allegedly powerful national issues like
slavery and secession were blunted by traditional patterns of ethno-

---

[21] For examples of works in this Nichols tradition see: Philip
S. Klein, Pennsylvania Politics, 1817-1832; A Game Without Rules
(Harrisburg, 1940); Charles McCool Snyder, The Jacksonian Heritage-
Pennsylvania Politics 1833-1848 (Harrisburg, 1958); and John F. Coleman,
"The Disruption of the Pennsylvania Democracy, 1848-1860", (Unpublished
Ph.D. dissertation, Pennsylvania State University, 1970), Erwin S.
Bradley, The Triumph of Militant Republicanism, A Study of Pennsylvania
and Presidential Politics, 1860-1872 (Philadelphia, 1964); and Frank
Evans, Pennsylvania Politics 1872-1877: A Study in Political Leadership
(Harrisburg, 1966).

[22] William G. Shade, "Pennsylvania Politics in the Jacksonian
Period: A Case Study, Northampton County, 1824-1844", Pennsylvania History,
XXXIX (July, 1972), pp. 313-333; Roger B. Petersen, "The Reaction to a
Heterogeneous Society: A Behavioral and Quantitative Analysis of Northern
Voting Behavior, 1845-1870, Pennsylvania as a Test Case," (Unpublished
Ph.D. dissertation, University of Pittsburgh, 1970); Michael Fitzgibbon
Holt, Forging a Majority: The Formation of the Republican Party in
Pittsburgh, 1848-1860 (New Haven, 1969).

religious voting. Major shifts in the American political system, they
argue, derived from the reorientation of the relationship between such
groups.

Interpretations of political behavior in Pennsylvania during
the mid-nineteenth century have been as wide ranging as those concerning
national politics. Some historians have viewed economic conflict as
the prime factor upon which Pennsylvania politics was based. Others have
modified the simplistic "rich versus poor" theme quite significantly by
studying political machines or specific voting units. Finally, a few
historians, following the lead of Lee Benson, have discounted economic
factors and detailed a political structure predicated upon the primacy
of ethno-religious tensions and tradition.

Schuylkill County, located in the southern sector of Pennsylvania's
anthracite district, reflected the economic and ethno-religious tensions
naturally associated with a developing mining area. The very rich and the
deplorably poor resided in the county; some were Protestants from England
and Wales, others solid German Lutherans, and many, particularly in the
latter part of the period under examination, were Roman Catholics from
Ireland. In brief, studying voting patterns in the county offers a chance
to test the validity of the conflicting interpretations on voting behavior.

During the entire period covered in this study, political
allegiances in Schuylkill County were related to economic factors. However, it seems apparent that at the same time ethno-religious differences served to polarize the county's voters. This meant that the political parties of Schuylkill County were not broad coalitions supporting

electoral machines totally devoid of any significant social differences;
nor, were they organizations which appealed simply to specific economic
groupings.

Even Wayne Broehl, who emphasized the economic aspects of the
Molly Maguire movement, conceded that ethno-religious factors contributed
significantly to the potency of the Mollies. Broehl stated in the
conclusion of his study:

> The ethnic dimensions of the Molly Maguire story
> are probably far more important than previously considered...
> In eastern Pennsylvania,...it was the Irish versus English
> and Welsh.[23]

In the context of the preceding three decades the Molly
Maguires must be seen as militant Irish Catholics who resented Protestant
domination of the society and culture as well as the economic order.
They were a reflection of basic ethno-religious tensions which were
becoming increasingly prevalent in Schuylkill County. These factors
emerged in the county between 1844 and 1872 and came to effect all
aspects of political behavior. They set the scene and drew the political
battle lines that hardened in the depression of the 1870's and erupted
into violence.

---

[23] Broehl, The Molly Maguires, p. 360.

Chapter I

Schuylkill County Pennsylvania, 1844-1872

Schuylkill County is located in the eastern portion of
Pennsylvania and has been generally associated in the minds of most
people with coal mining, the Molly Maguires and labor unrest. However, this geographically diversified area offered social and religious
contrasts which made the county an example of the effect of ethno-
religious forces upon nineteenth century politics. Situated about
thirty miles north of Reading, one hundred miles northwest of Philadelphia,
and fifty miles south of the Wilkes-Barre-Scranton area, it comprised
the southern sector of Pennsylvania's vast hard-coal district.[1]
Dauphin and Lebanon Counties bordered Schuylkill on the west, with
Northumberland and Columbia Counties to the north, Luzerne and Northampton Counties on the east and Berks and Lehigh Counties to the south.

The topography of Schuylkill County is varied and rugged
as that of any other county in the state of Pennsylvania, consisting
essentially of a succession of hills, valleys and mountain chains
running northeasterly in a nearly parallel fashion across the entire
length of the county.[2] The south western portion is the only non-
mountainous sector of the county; and it contained some of Pennsylvania's
most lucrative and productive farms during the middle of the nineteenth

---

[1] In 1860, a trip to Philadelphia and back by train consumed
nearly a whole day. Today, a two hour drive separates Pottsville,
Schuylkill's county seat, and Philadelphia.

[2] History of Schuylkill County, Pennsylvania (New York, 1881),
p. 32. No editor of this work is given. Since the publisher was
W.W. Munsell it will be subsequently referred to as Munsell, History.

century.[3] These agricultural districts grew and prospered along
with the rapidly expanding urban mining areas which clustered near
the geographic center of the county.

Numerous streams cut across the county, several of which
were partially navigable; and the average rainfall in the county equals
or exceeds that in most of the state.[4] Yet this abundant water supply
was difficult to utilize, because of the wild torrential nature of the
mountain streams. The water resources of the county were most useful
in cleaning coal and carrying on commerce.

Like most of the state's mining areas, Schuylkill County
possessed an imposing mountain structure. These rocky, erosion scarred
peaks, which rose to as high as seventeen hundred feet above sea level,
were usually paralleled by less defined slopes. Between these mountains
and hills were located the productive valleys which so heavily influenced
the county's economy and its population growth. These geographic factors
were complemented by an awesome ridge system which connected the mountains
and hills and crisscrossed the valleys.[5]

---

[3] The southern and western portions of Schuylkill County still
are valuable farm areas and boast of having remained a prosperous area
typified by independent, relatively small farms.

[4] Munsell, History, p. 32.

[5] Ibid., p. 34.

Three mountain chains intersected the county. Blue Mountain, also known as the Kittatinny Mountain, was the southernmost of these ranges and represented the extension into Pennsylvania of the Blue Ridge. This chain was broken only by the Schuylkill River near the site of Port Clinton, which became vital to the canal trade. The two other chains running parallel to Blue Mountain were Second Mountain, not an overwhelming geographic factor, and the more pronounced Sharp Mountain still farther north. Two other mountains, Broad and Locust, were generally considered mere arms of the Sharp Mountain. While Blue Mountain had but one gap, at Port Clinton, Second Mountain and Sharp Mountain together possessed thirteen clearly passable natural gateways.

The major streams of the county flowed into three drainage systems--the Susquehanna, the Schuylkill and the Lehigh. The Schuylkill was most influential in the middle portion of the county; the Lehigh drained the county's eastern portions and the Susquehanna most influenced the northern and western sectors of Schuylkill County. As noted previously, the streams of the county afforded the basic means of coal transport through much of the period under consideration.[6] Even when the railroad began seriously to challenge the canal, many tracks ran closely parallel to the old waterways simply because of the necessity of taking advantage of the gaps which penetrated Schuylkill County's otherwise solid wall of mountain barriers.

---

[6] The Schuylkill Navigation System served the coal transporters of the county. Unless otherwise noted, a reference to the "canal" means the Schuylkill System. A further discussion of the canal is found later in this chapter.

When the county was officially created in 1811, it contained nine farming townships--Brunswick, Schuylkill, Manheim, Norwegian, Upper and Lower Mahantongo and Pine Grove from Berks County, and West Penn and Rush from Northampton County.[7] Eventually Brunswick split into two townships as did Manheim. By 1853 Lower Mahantongo had disappeared entirely, becoming part of Hubley, Hegins, Porter and Frailey Townships.[8]

The major towns of the county were all incorporated by 1872. On the whole, the towns came into existence after the townships were well established because of the relative lateness of the anthracite booms in specific areas of the county. These booms usually initiated the formation of new boroughs. By 1867, twenty boroughs were officially created in the county. Of these, fifteen were located in or near the coal districts of Schuylkill County. However, Pine Grove Borough was nestled among the farm acres that comprised the southwestern extremity of Schuylkill County. Schuylkill Haven, Cressona, Auburn, Orwigsburg and Port Clinton were situated in the agriculturally oriented southern tier of the county and stretched five to fifteen miles south of the county seat, Pottsville, which was very near the geographic center of the county.

---

[7] Herwood Hobbs, "The Origin of the Names of Towns and Townships in Schuylkill County," Publications of the Historical Society of Schuylkill County, VI (1947), p. 43.

[8] Ibid., p. 44.

Table I-A

Economic Grouping of Schuylkill County Townships and Boroughs, 1840, 1870

1840 Occupational Orientation

	%Mining	%Agriculture	%Business	%Navigation	%Professional
Barry	–	82	17	–	1
Branch	83	7	9	–	1
Minersville	64	–	33	1	2
East Brunswick	4	93	2	1	–
Lower Mahantango	5	85	9	–	1
Manheim	–	54	30	14	2
Orwigsburg	–	14	64	10	12
Pine Grove	14	64	17	4	1
Pottsville	31	1	57	6	5
Rush	–	86	14	–	–
Schuylkill	72	10	18	–	–
Tamaqua	9	68	20	–	3
Union	–	99	–	1	–
Upper Mahantango	–	91	8	–	1
Wayne	–	88	9	3	–
West Brunswick	10	89	1	–	–
West Penn	–	98	–	2	–

1870 Occupational Orientation

Farm Townships	Farm Oriented Boroughs	Mining Townships	Mining-oriented Boroughs
Barry	Auburn	Blythe	Ashland
East Brunswick	Cressona	Branch	Mahanoy City
Eldred	Orwigsburg	Butler	Middleport
Hegins	Pine Grove Borough	Cass	Minersville
Hubley	Port Clinton	East Norwegian	Mount Carbon
North Manheim	Sch. Haven	Frailey	Port Carbon
Pine Grove		Foster	Pottsville
Porter		Mahanoy Twp.	St. Clair
Rahn		New Castle	Shenandoah
Ryan		Norwegian	Tamaqua
South Manheim		Reilly	Tremont Borough
Union		Rush	Yorkville
Upper Mahantongo		Schuylkill	
Washington		Tremont Twp.	
Wayne			
West Brunswick			
West Penn			

The initial population of Schuylkill County was composed
primarily of German farmers who drifted north from neighboring Berks,
and settled in the county's richest farm area which soon became known
as the "red barn" or "Dutch" region.[9] The less penetrable and less
fertile mountainous sections of the county were not developed until
the later anthracite coal booms. When the search for the valued "black
diamonds" necessitated the opening of the rugged coal regions of the
county, settlement generally took place in the valleys which were
found at the base of the mountain slopes. The geography of the area
dictated that these valley anthracite settlements would be isolated
from each other, as well as from the agriculturally-oriented zones of
the county.

Hence, Schuylkill County was composed of "islands" of settlement, geographically separated by the mountain ridges which bisected
the county. Virtually all of these areas were devoted wholly to either
farming or mining. Not a single township could claim both a well
developed farm and anthracite enterprise. Where mines existed, farm-
lands simply did not.

Schuylkill County can be described clearly by dividing it into
four types of economic districts: farming townships, farming-oriented
boroughs, mining townships and mining-oriented boroughs. Such an
economic pattern meant that isolated, homogeneous population groupings

---

[9] The Germans of the county are still referred to as Dutchmen.
They were associated with conservative, well painted barns which were
often red and decorated with symbolic hex signs.

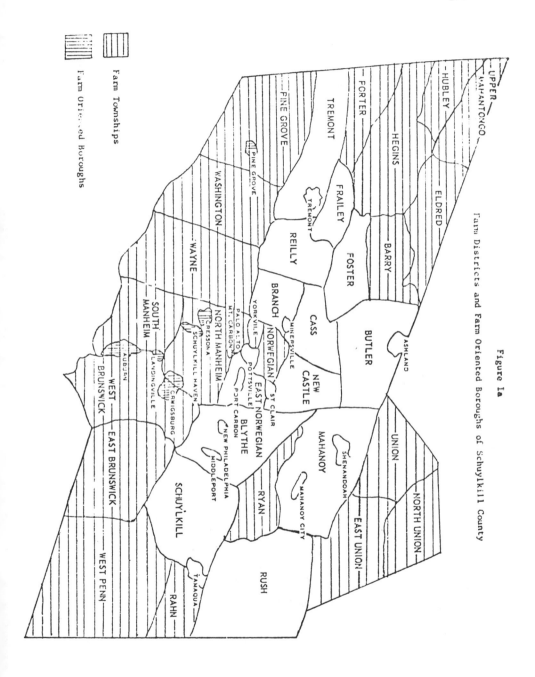

Figure Ia

Farm Districts and Farm Oriented Boroughs of Schuylkill County

would be the rule rather than the exception in mid-nineteenth century
Schuylkill County because specific types of people would move into
these clearly defined economic areas. However, the geographical pattern
which set farmers and miners apart also separated people who were of
different ethno-religious backgrounds.

The economic development of the county, at first predicated
solely upon agriculture, proceeded at a lazy pace until the mid-1820s.
As late as 1828, a speculator who traveled over the future boundaries
of Schuylkill County reported passing only three crude dwellings in a
journey of thirty-five miles.[10] However, the transformation of the
county's had already begun. The county entered a new era at the end
of 1824 when the completion of the Schuylkill Navigations Company's
major line opened the county's vast anthracite resources to commercial
development.[11] This canal system led to the rapid maturation of the
coal trade which in turn started a tide of speculation that closely
resembled the gold rushes into California and the Klondike. By the
end of the decade the county was yielding half of the hard coal tonnage
of the United States.[12]

---

[10] Clifton Yearley, Enterprise and Anthracite-Economics and
Democracy in Schuylkill County 1820-1875 (Baltimore, 1961), p. 24.

[11] For the story of the early canal trade development see
H. Benjamin Powell, "Pennsylvania's Transportation Policy 1825-1828,"
Pennsylvania History, XXXVIII (April, 1971) pp. 134-151. Also see
Walter Sanderlin, "The Expanding Horizons of the Schuylkill Navigation
Company, 1815-1870," Pennsylvania History, XXXVI (April, 1969), pp.
174-191.

[12] Yearley, Enterprise and Anthracite, p. 15.

Table I-B

Population Growth of Schuylkill County

	Population	% Increase
1820	11,339	
		83
1830	20,744	
		40
1840	29,053	
		109
1850	60,713	
		47
1860	89,510	
		30
1870	116,428	

Table I-C

Estimated Percentage of the Population of Major Ethnic Groups

	1850	1860	1870
Germans	45	35	32
English and Welsh	35	35	32
Irish	15	25	30
Others	5	5	5

Pottsville, in the heart of the mining area, became the mecca for the usual gathering of nascent capitalists and the more corrupt characters normally attracted to boom areas. Pottsville's incredible growth paralleled similar developments in the other mining sections of the county, but in that town alone the number of permanent buildings increased sixfold in the three years between 1826 and 1829.[13] The county continued to grow through the 1830's when the boom conditions were given a further stimulus with the advent of railroading in the region. The first primitive rail lines were opened in the county as early as 1829, but rail construction attained notable levels during the 1830's. Two significant lines, the Mt. Carbon, and the Little Schuylkill, commenced full scale operations prior to 1833.[14] But the real dawning of the railroad era in the county began in January of 1842 when the Philadelphia and Reading Railroad officially reached Pottsville and the heart of the anthracite region. This quite naturally precipitated an immediate reduction in the cost of coal transport and consequently made hard coal economically available to the people residing in concentrated population centers like Reading and Philadelphia.

The year 1842 also marked the beginning of economic dominance in the county by the Philadelphia and Reading Coal and Iron Company (or the Reading Company). For the next thirty years, the Reading battled against the spirit of individual enterprise which was so firmly entrenched

---

[13] Yearley, _Enterprise and Anthracite_, p. 15.

[14] Munsell, _History_, p. 46.

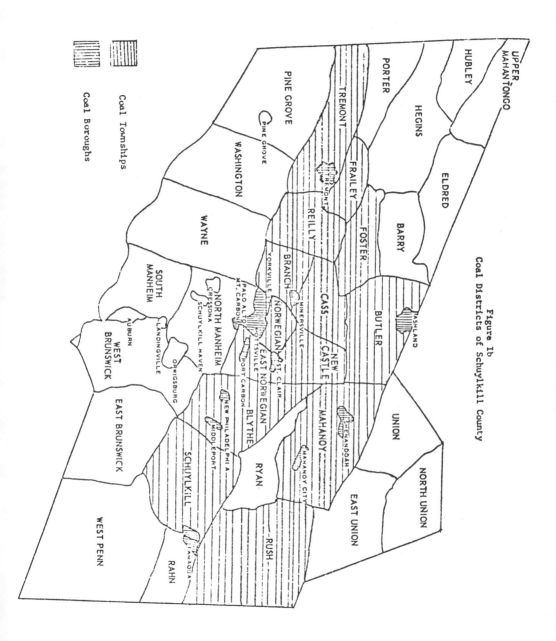

Figure Ib
Coal Districts of Schuylkill County

in Schuylkill County. Most county residents vehemently opposed the
consolidation of the private collieries, because this ran counter to
the general trends in the other coal areas of the state.[15] The Reading
Company, however, gradually bought out individual operators until in
1871 it achieved a virtual monopoly of Schuylkill County's anthracite
business.

The man most responsible for the demise of the individual
operators in the county was Franklin B. Gowen, who organized the Reading
Company in the area and led the battle against the individual operators.
At first, he gained the friendship of mine laborers by offering written
contracts and company benefits in all Reading Company collieries.[16]
After weakening individual owners by winning the confidence of the miners,
Gowen abandoned his "progressive" stance toward labor and concentrated solely
on enriching himself and the Reading Company.[17]

This rapid economic development which took place in the county
between the late 1820's and the early 1870's caused an equally rapid
population growth which drastically altered the ethno-religious composition

---

[15] George Korson, Black Rock (Baltimore, 1960), p. 89.

[16] Marvin Schlegel, Ruler of the Reading: The Life of
Franklin B. Gowen, 1836-1889 (Harrisburg, 1947), passim.

[17] Gowen was an active county Democrat, but he was also the
man who hired the Pinkerton Detective Agency to infiltrate and destroy
the alleged Molly Maguire organization.

of the region.[18] What was until the 1820's nearly a homogeneously
Pennsylvania "Dutch" county suddenly received an influx of anthracite
miners from other areas of Europe. The first of these newcomers to
appear in significant numbers were the Welsh and English, people who
had acquired basic mining skills in their homelands. These groups
had arrived throughout the 1830's and 1840's in large numbers and then
their influx tapered off as the Civil War approached. During the 1830's
the county's population rose 40% owing largely to this immigration from
the British Isles.

The final group to be attracted to the county by the lucrative
mining enterprise were the Irish Catholics who left their homeland in
great numbers during the famines and political unrest between 1840 and 1860.
During these years the population of Schuylkill County rose an amazing
200%, increasing from roughly 30,000 inhabitants to 90,000. Many of the
newcomers who arrived during these years were the Irish Catholics. No
other major ethnic element entered the area in significant numbers prior
to 1872; and the county, thus, broke down into four distinct groups: the
Germans, the Irish, the Welsh and the English.[19] The Germans were largely

---

[18] The best concise discussion of the anthracite region's social
structure can be found in Rowland Berthoff, "The Social Order of the Anthracite
Region, 1825–1902," Pennsylvania Magazine of History and Biography, LXXXIX
(July, 1965), pp. 261–291. Berthoff's book, British Immigrants in Industrial
America (New York, 1953), is also highly useful in detailing Welsh and English
immigration.

[19] A scattered group of Scotch and Scotch-Irish, German Catholics,
and French entered the region, but none of their groups was ever significant.
Of these groups, only the German Catholics founded places of worship any-
where in the county. The Black population in the county never approached
1% of its total.

farmers and lived in the productive southern and western districts of the county.[20] The English and Welsh were predominantly miners who settled in the urban coal regions of the county. Pottsville, Minersville, Port Carbon and Llewellyn quickly acquired large Welsh and English populations. The Irish, who could find work only in mining areas, also lived in the coal towns and townships of the county. Areas like Cass Township, just north of Pottsville, had become an Irish enclave by the 1850's. The Irish also settled in the mining boroughs like Pottsville, Minersville, and St. Clair, which were located close to the major collieries. Forced to live relatively close to their traditional Welsh enemies caused natural animosities to develop.[21]

This bitterness among the Irish Catholics and the English and Welsh was aggravated by the fact that normally the Protestants were the foremen in the mines. Throughout the whole of the nineteenth century, the Irish of the county remained predominately miners. At first, the inexperience of the non-Irish miners justified such a situation, but later the hierarchy was maintained simply because non-Catholic mine owners and their lower level managers discriminated against the Irish.

Throughout the turbulent period between 1844 and 1872 most of the Germans lived in an undisturbed, homogeneous society. No Irish were attracted to the farm sectors of the county and the Welsh and English who migrated to the region came to dig hard coal and not till the soil.

---

[20] Some Germans mined, especially early in the development of the coal trade, but they were quickly thrust aside by the English, Welsh, and Irish. For a discussion of German mining pioneers see Korson, Black Rock, pp. 102-108.

[21] Alan Conway (ed.), The Welsh in America (Minneapolis, 1961), p. 168.

Table I-D

Native Born Percentages in Subdivisions of Schuylkill County, 1870*

Upper Mahantongo	100
West Penn	99
West Brunswick	99
Hegins	99
Washington	99
Eldred	98
Hubley	98
Pine Grove Township	97
Wayne	97
Orwisburg	97
Pine Grove Borough	96
East Brunswick	96
South Manheim	96
Union	95
Barry	93
Port Clinton	92
Cressona	91
Schuylkill Haven	90
Ryan	89
Porter	86
North Manheim	81
Pottsville	78
Frailey	75
Tremont	74
Branch	73
Tamaqua	73
Schuylkill Township	71
Minersville	68
Ashland	66
Blythe	66
Norwegian	65
New Castle	64
East Norwegian	63
Rush	63
Cass	62
Foster	62
Butler	61
St. Clair	60
Reilly	59
Mahanoy Township	58
Shenandoah	57

*The foreign born percentage of the county was 30% in 1860 and 26% in 1870.

Consequently, the German farmers who still constructed large, well painted barns, strongly resisted mixing with their mining neighbors. They continued to speak their native language, and prided themselves on their frugality, traditionalism, and economic independence.[22] The county Germans never quite trusted the modernity which was associated with the county's coal regions. This skepticism long characterized most Pennsylvania German farmers.[23]

The clannish Germans of the county were largely Lutheran with a small minority belonging to the Reformed Church. These were the "Church" Germans and not the "sect" Germans like Moravians, Mennonites, Amish and Schwenkfelders or the various Wesleyan groups.[24] The "Church people" emphasized an institutionalized religion and thus gave considerable attention to matters such as grace, the sacraments, an official clergy, and the proper religious education of children.[25] The "sect" Germans lacked the dogmatic rigidity of their churched counterparts; instead, they gave preference to individualism in religion. The "sect" Germans,

---

[22] Russell W. Gilbert, A Picture of Pennsylvania Germans (Gettysburg, 1947), p. 42.

[23] Ibid., p. 41.

[24] The best discussion of "Church" and "sect" Germans can be found in the January, 1942 edition of Pennsylvania History. See H.M.J. Klein, "The Church People in Colonial Pennsylvania," Pennsylvania History IX (January, 1942), pp. 37-47; Raymond Albright, "The Sect People in Colonial Pennsylvania," Pennsylvania History, IX (January, 1942), pp. 48-53. (The articles are further discussed on pages 54 and 55 of the same journal in relation to their presentation to the Pennsylvania Historical Association.)

[25] H.M.J. Klein, "The Church People", p. 37.

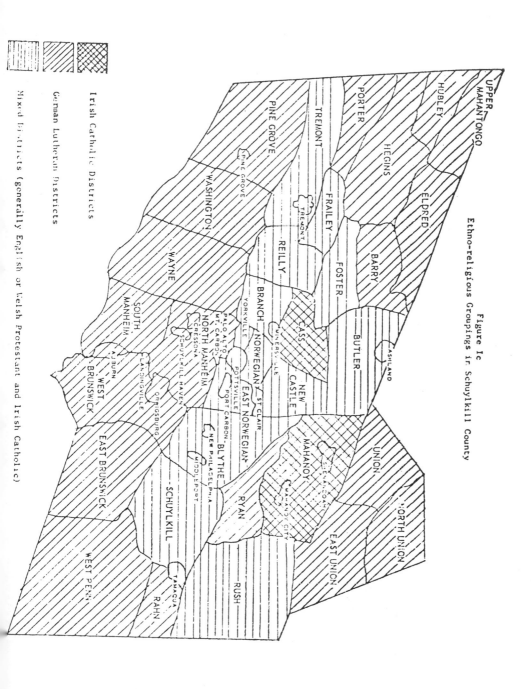

Figure Ic

Ethno-religious Groupings in Schuylkill County

tended to dissent from "Church" doctrine,[26] and opposed the ritualism
of the established churches.[27]

The "Church" Germans of the county and the Irish Catholics
could be categorized as "doctrinally orthodox."[28] Sociologist Gerhard
Lenski has defined "doctrinal orthodoxy" as the "orientation which
stresses intellectual assent to prescribed doctrines."[29] This refers
to a passive, consenting religious style which enables followers to
successfully compartmentalize their secular and religious lives. The
ritualism and institutionalized formalities associated with "doctrinal
orthodoxy" have led some scholars to describe this approach as "high
Church".[30] Both the German Lutherans and Irish Catholics relied on
established Churches and clergy and rejected individualistic religious
practices. German Lutheran services resembled the Catholic Mass far
more than the services of Methodists or Presbyterians. This difference
was reflected in the Catholic and Lutheran use of the sacraments and
adherence to transubstantiation rather than consubstantiation.

---

[26] Albright, "The Sect People", p. 48.

[27] Ibid., p. 52. (The Irish Catholics were "Church" people in
the sense that they, too, emphasized formalisms such as an official clergy,
elaborate rituals, and the sacraments.)

[28] Gerhard Lenski, The Religious Factor. A Sociological Study
of Religion's Impact on Politics, Economics, and Family Life (New York,
1961), p. 25.

[29] Ibid.

[30] Richard Jensen, "The Religious and Occupational Roots of
Party Identification: Illinois and Indiana in the 1870's," Civil War
History, XVI (December, 1970), pp. 325-343.

The "doctrinally orthodox" groups also rejected attempts to
reform society by religious means which resented the mixing of religion
and politics in general. Within the context of nineteenth century America
the groups who had exemplified the close relation between Church and State
in Europe set themselves against such intimate relations between religion
and politics. They refused to become moralizers or crusading zealots.
Religion existed clearly apart from politics in the lives of these people.[31]
This attitude manifested itself quite clearly in Schuylkill County; for
example, German Lutherans and the Irish Catholics gave little support to
either the temperance or sabbatarian movements during the mid-nineteenth
century. The German Lutherans were the only non-Catholic group to actively
oppose the nativist movement of the period. Their formal religions also
dictated that they both resist common education and defend parochial
schools through which their young could be properly trained.

The English and, more specifically, the Welsh who were generally
Presbyterians or Methodists, tended toward what Lenski termed "devotionalism" in their religious style. He defined as "devotionalist" those
denominations which emphasize the "importance of private, or personal,
communion with God."[32] Devotionalists" practice a more active style of
religion than the "doctrinally orthodox" and tend to be more receptive to
politico-religious crusades like temperance and sabbatarianism. In
county politics, these religious groups supplied the backbone of all
reform activities.

---

[31] Albright, "The Sect People", p. 51.

[32] Lenski, Religious Factor, p. 25.

The ethno-religious structure of the county can easily be aligned along an "orthodox" and "devotionalist" spectrum. The most "doctrinally orthodox" ethnic element was the Irish who were over-whelmingly Roman Catholic. Although they were for the most part Lutheran or Reformed, the county's Germans included a small group of Catholics and a larger minority devoted to the German-speaking Wesleyan sects such as the United Brethren and the Evangelical Association, who were oriented toward the "devotionalist" end of the spectrum. The English element was also religiously mixed. They ranged from a handful of Lutherans through a sizable number of Episcopalians to Methodism with a smattering of Presbyterians and Baptists. Finally the Welsh could be found at the extreme "devotionalist" end of the spectrum including "new school" Presbyterians, Methodists, Baptists and the county's only Congregationalists.[33]

Geographically, the county divided into nearly homogenous ethno-religious areas. The German Lutheran townships were clearly distinct from the remainder of the county and agriculturally oriented. The boroughs of this area were originally heavily German Lutheran as well; however, they gradually acquired an influx of English and Welsh and assumed a more cosmopolitan ethno-religious character as the century wore on. The mining areas of the county had far fewer Germans and a clear majority of English and Welsh Protestants. It was into the mining

---

[33] This is based on the social statistics schedule from manuscript Seventh United States Census (1850); Munsell, History, pp. 181-390 and I. Daniel Rupp, History of Northampton, Lehigh, Monroe, Carbon and Schuylkill Counties (Harrisburg, 1845), pp. 249-271.

townships and boroughs that the increasing segment of Irish moved to
rub elbows and noses with their traditional rivals from the Old Country.
In these hetrogenious districts the tension existing between ethno-
religious groups were most intense. Finally as the Irish population
grew, wholly Irish Catholic townships like Cass and Mahanoy appeared.

These ethno-religious contrasts within Schuylkill County
obviously influenced the political situation in the region. This is
not to deny the influence of economic differences in a county which was
composed of distinct economic groupings and notorious for clear instances
of class conflict. To a certain extent, economic matters did wield a
degree of political potency in the county, but the impact of ethno-
religious discord transcended that of socioeconomic difference in
importance. The political milieu in the county can be fully understood
only when the ethno-religious factor is adequately examined. As long
as the Democrats remained the party of the "doctrinally orthodox,"
they were the unchallenged rulers of the area. The main task of their
Whig and Republican rivals was to destroy this coalition; and, whatever
their differences were, neither the Whigs nor the Republicans could
accomplish this between 1844 and 1872.[34]

---

[34] The Democrats lost permanent control of the county during
the politically volatile 1890's when the German Lutherans finally
abandoned the party. The Democrats have won few elections in the
county since the turn of the century.

Chapter II

Mass Voting Behavior in Schuylkill County, 1844-1872

Schuylkill County was strongly Democratic throughout most of the nineteenth century. At no time was this tendency more pronounced than during the first three decades of the county's existence. In its formative, agriculturally oriented years, Schuylkill County's overwhelming Democratic majorities were made up almost entirely of the German Lutheran farmers who originally inhabited the county.[1] The development of the coal trade attracted people of English, Welsh and eventually, Irish lineage and ushered in the first period of two party competition in county history. Rapid economic growth and cultural diversification characterized these years and effected the county's political parties in complex ways which have eluded traditional historians. Political conflict became rooted in the differences between ethnoreligious groups.

A. Democrats Versus Whigs, 1844-1852

In the years before 1838 Schuylkill County generally produced lopsided Democratic victories. In his three campaigns for the presidency, Andrew Jackson gained 94%, 80% and 73% of the county's votes and gubernatorial candidates often did as well. However, political parties were not well developed during these years. Voter turnout seldom exceeded 50% of the white adult males; and as elsewhere in the country, Schuylkill County's voters took more interest in state than national elections

_____

[1] Approximately 65% of the county was German Lutheran until the coal boom in the 1840's. It must be kept in mind that Schuylkill County was once homogeneously agricultural.

(Figure II-a).[2] During these pre-party years, there was little relation between behavior in state and national elections. Democrat George Wolf carried the county in 1829, 1832 and again in 1835, but there was only a modest correlation between his vote and that for Jackson.[3]

After 1838 two comparatively modern parties emerged in Schuylkill County. The Democratic majority that had been steadily declining stabilized and the voting patterns evident in national elections were closely reflected in gubernatorial contests. Turnout rose; and, in contrast to the earlier years, national elections featured greater voter interest than state elections.[4] For fifteen years Schuylkill County exhibited a stable two-party system in which the Whigs struggled to unseat the dominant Democrats.

In the ten fall elections held in the county between 1844 and 1853, the Democrats emerged victorious seven times.[5] The Whigs received better than 50% of the vote only in 1846, 1847 and 1848.[6] The election

---

[2] Shade, "Jacksonian Period Politics," pp. 316-17.

[3] The correlation between the 1832 gubernatorial and presidential elections was $r_s=.45$ which is not significant at .01 level.

[4] The correlation between the 1838 gubernatorial election and the 1840 presidential election is $r_s=.87$; and for the two elections in 1844, it is $r_s=.89$.

[5] All election results, unless otherwise specified, were taken from official results published in the Miners' Journal.

[6] The Democratic percentages during the decade ran as follows:

1844 - 57%	1849 - 51%
1845 - 65%	1850 - 51%
1846 - 47%	1851 - 54%
1847 - 46%	1852 - 54%
1848 - 43%	1853 - 55%

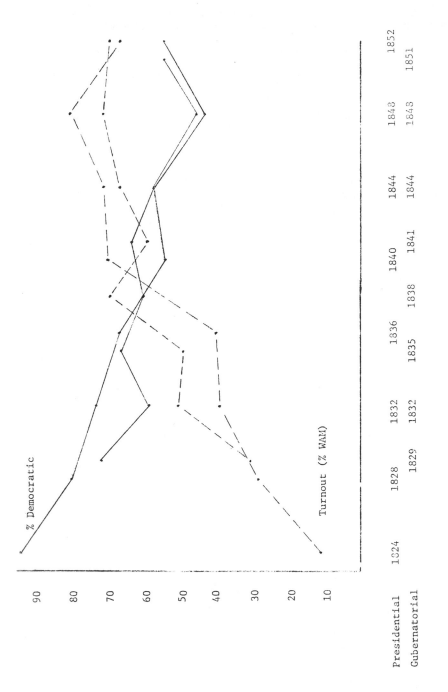

Figure II-a Presidential and Gubernatorial Elections in Schuylkill County, 1824-1852

of 1844 was a "maintaining" election which continued past political patterns.[7] The elections of 1846, 1847 and 1848 "deviated" from the previous "normal vote" in the county; however, the permanent restructuring of the political organizations also took place as a result of these three elections. Therefore, 1846 could be more properly termed a "realigning" election. The year 1849 saw the altered parties return to a new period of Democratic control. The elections of 1850, 1851, 1852, and 1853 maintained this Democratic hegemony, but the new Democratic coalition differed in several particulars from the organization which had controlled the county until 1846.[8]

The election of 1844, nationally, saw James K. Polk become the third man to thwart Henry Clay's presidential ambitions. Most historians have seen this election as the first major sectional contest in our history, because of the Democrats insistence on the "re-annexation of Texas" and the emergence of the abolitionist Liberty Party which drained enough New York votes away from Clay to cost him the electoral

---

[7] The terminology here is taken from Angus Campbell, et.al., The American Voter (New York, 1960), and Angus Campbell, "Surge and Decline: A Study of Electoral Change," Public Opinion Quarterly, XXIV (Fall, 1960), pp. 397-418. Campbell hesitated to apply his concepts to nineteenth century America but they seem to provide a useful analytical scheme.

[8] Campbell might have termed the election of 1849 as a "reinstating election" in that it returned the Democrats to power and ushered in a new maintaining period. However, the term is not applicable since the realigning election of 1846 restructured the political coalitions which had existed until 1846. For a discussion of this see Philip E. Converse, Angus Campbell, Warren Miller, Donald E. Stokes, "Stability and Change in 1960: A Reinstating Election," American Political Science Review, (June, 1961), pp. 269-280.

votes of the Empire State and the election.[9] This view typifies the
tendency of historians to treat elections autonomously and ascribe partisan
affiliation to national issues featured in campaign oratory and the way in
which the "Civil War synthesis" has warped traditional views of ante-bellum
politics.[10]

In Schuylkill County the election of 1844 followed the pattern
established in the late 1830s and neither Texas nor the slavery question
played a role in its outcome. Although the Democratic majority fluctuated
between 1840 and 1844, the introduction of the Texas issue had little
effect.[11] The Democrats carried 57% of the vote for Polk and their
local candidates, as the Whigs proved utterly incapable of making any
headway in the German Lutheran farm districts.[12] The Whigs

---

[9] For examples of interpretations emphasizing sectional differences and the Texas question see: Charles Wiltse, The New Nation, 1800–
1845 (New York, 1961); and Avery O. Craven, The Coming of the Civil War
(Chicago, 1966 ed.). Benson, Concept, pp. 254-67, challenges this view.

[10] For a review of the arguments see, Joel Silbey, "The Civil
War Synthesis in American History," Civil War History, X (June, 1964),
pp. 130-132.

[11] The correlation between 1841 gubernatorial and 1844 presidential
elections is $r_s = .72$. There was no liberty vote in the county; and the 1843
election was generally non-partisan.

[12] The Democratic leanings of German Lutherans are discussed in
many places including: Sharp, Jacksonians Versus the Banks, p. 326;
Robert Remini, The Election of Andrew Jackson (Philadelphia, 1963),
p. 104; Benson, Concept of Jacksonian Democracy, pp. 173-174; Shade,
"Jacksonian Period Politics", pp. 325-327; Peterson, "Reaction to a
Heterogeneous Society", p. 121.

were competitive only in those urban mining areas of the county where Welsh
and English Protestants resided like Pottsville, Mount Carbon, Port Carbon
and Minersville.[13]

Most of the issues which agitated the local political scene in
1844 had definite ethno-religious overtones. One such issue which clearly
differentiated the local parties was sabbatarianism. The Whigs firmly
supported Sunday laws. Bannan editorialized:

> The most powerful obstacle to the progress of
> morality is this prevalent disregard of the
> Sabbath, and it seems to us that no other single
> cause is so potent in counter-acting the influence
> of religious truth.[14]

The Whigs also condemned "foreign religious influences" and lamented the
fact the Irish Catholics voted blindly Democratic. In fact, the Whig
Miners' Journal ultimately blamed Clay's defeat in the county on the
"naturalized Catholic vote."[15] The county Whigs pursued this anti-Catholicism
further by advocating an extension of the naturalization period and stricter
enforcement of voting laws. Benjamin Bannan, the chief Whig spokesman and
editor of the Miners' Journal, even proposed that the Whigs assume a more
openly nativistic stance in future local elections.[16]

---

[13]Benson, Concept, pp. 167-69 comments on the Whiggish tendency
of the Welsh.

[14]Miners' Journal, November 16, 1844, p. 2.

[15]Ibid.

[16]Ibid.

The Democrats, conversely, refused to support sabbatarianism, opposed extending the naturalization period, pleaded for "tolerance in religion and politics," rejected nativist schemes against the foreign born and vowed to defend the county's aliens and Roman Catholics.[17] The Democrats constantly stated that prejudice and intolerance would eventually tear down the American governmental structure.

The only economic issue to receive wide attention in local politics during the 1844 campaign was the tariff question.[18] However, both local parties strongly supported high protection and their positions on the tariff question did not clearly set them apart. The Democrats claimed to be the tariff party and vowed never to support free trade. They accused Henry Clay and other national Whigs of having unclear tariff views.[19] The local Whigs also assumed the guise of the county's "tariff party" and called the tariff the key issue of the 1844 campaign "at all levels."[20] Bannan even argued that Whig tariff programs made them the party of the common man.[21] A great deal of editorial ink was spilled over the tariff question with each party

---

[17]Pottsville Emporium and Colliers' Democratic Register, June 29, 1844, p. 2. (This paper will hereafter be cited as the Emporium.)

[18]Snyder, Jacksonian Heritage, pp. 171-186, emphasized the importance of the tariff question during the election of 1844 in Pennsylvania.

[19]Emporium, July 13, 1844, p. 2.

[20]Miners' Journal, March 30, 1844, p. 2.

[21]Ibid.

trying to appear more zealous than its opponent in support of the
protective principle.

Sectional issues were noticeably absent from the campaign
rhetoric in Schuylkill County. Not a single mention was made of the
Liberty Party, nor did it receive a single vote locally. The expansion
issue clearly aroused no stormy political passions in the county. The
Texas question and Polk's expansionist proclivities received only passing
approval in the Democratic press and minor disapproval from the Miners'
Journal.

The questions which divided the parties the 1844 election in
Schuylkill County were sabbatarianism, nativism and anti-Catholicism,
issues which tended to polarize the devotionalists and religiously
orthodox of the county. Democrats and Whigs basically agreed on the
leading economic issue of the day. No issue peculiar to the election
of 1844 in Schuylkill County caused any significant shift in the traditional voting habits of its residents. The outcome maintained the
political pattern set in the mid-1830s. Henry Clay lost Schuylkill
County, not because of Texas or the Liberty Party, but because German
Lutherans farmers voted heavily against him and for the party of ethno-
religious toleration.

The importance of these differences can be seen by closely
examining the voting patterns in the county in 1844. As Table II-A
shows the traditional hypothesis which associates wealth and Whiggery

Table II-A

1844 Ranking of Schuylkill County Minor Civil Divisions
on Four Variables*

	Party (1)	Wealth (2)	Religion (3)	Agriculture (4)
Mahantongoes	1	13	2	3
Union	2	15	6	1
West Penn	3	2	3	2
Rush	4	21	7	5
Wayne	5	6	1	4
Orwigsburg	6	17	11	15
Barry	7	16	8	6
Pine Grove Twp.	8**	12	10	11
West Brunswick	9	19	9	8***
Schuylkill Haven	10	18	17	14
Schuylkill Twp.	11	4	13	16
Tamaqua	12	1	15	10
Pine Grove Bo.	13	10	14	12
Branch	14	9	18	18
Blythe	15	8	19	17
East Brunswick	16	14	4	7***
Porter	17	20	5	9****
Manheims	18	7	12	13
Minersville	19	5	21	21
E. Norwegian	20	3	16	19
Pottsville	21	11	20	20

$\text{Gamma}_{1.2} = -.179$ $\text{Gamma}_{1.3} = .521$ $\text{Gamma}_{1.4} = .617$

*The four variables used here are: Party--a ranking of constituencies
from the highest to the lowest in percent Democratic based on
Appendix A; Wealth-- a ranking from the highest to the lowest in terms
of per capita "True Valuation" of wealth from Schedule 6, "Social
Statistics," in the manuscript 1850 United States Census for
Pennsylvania; Religion--a ranking of constituencies from the highest
to the lowest on a scale of "doctrinal orthodoxy" based upon proportion
of church seats from Schedule 6, "Social Statistics," in the manuscript
1850 United States Census for Pennsylvania; and Agriculture--a ranking
of constituencies from those with the highest percentage of farmers to
those with the lowest from Sixth Census...1840 (Washington: 1841).
**Based upon the 1848 and 1852 division of the vote between the
township and the borough.
***Based upon an estimate of what the working population should have
been assuming that only the number of farmers reported is incorrect.
****Estimated by taking 1/6 of the farmers and all of the miners
from Lower Mahantongo.
*****With this number of cases a Gamma=.410 or above is considered
statistically significant at .01 level of probability.

did not hold in Schuylkill County where there was in fact <u>correlation</u>

<u>between</u> <u>wealth</u> <u>and</u> <u>the</u> Democratic vote. Occupationally the pattern was

rather confused. Neither the rank of areas by level of commercial and

business activity nor that for mining <u>per se</u> correlates with Whig voting.[22]

However, there was a strong positive association between farming areas and

centers of Democratic dominence. The rural areas did give far greater

support to the Democratic party than to the Whigs. These were the areas

of old German Lutheran settlement which were now politically juxtaposed

to the newer areas oriented toward mining and populated predominantly by

English and Welsh newcomers to the county. Consequently there is also a

strong and positive correlation between Democratic strength the rank on the

scale of "doctrinal orthodoxy."

Any attempt to statistically weigh the relative importance of these

two variables is stymied by the crude measures used here and a problem of

missing data. Nine of the top ten farm townships were 100% German Lutheran

and Reformed with the tenth being basically so, but containing a single

United Brethren congregation. The ranking used here is based upon the per

cent of the population accounted by Lutheran and Reformed Church seats, and

the statistic used is sensitive to ordinal differences. Within this group

our order may not reflect the "real" order of these areas. Secondly, the

1840 census for two townships—the Brunswicks—is clearly wrong and our

estimates may have altered the "real" order on the farming scale as well. If

one ignores the Brunswicks, the correlation between Democratic voting and

doctrinal orthodoxy becomes higher than that between the percentage of farmers

and Democratic voting.

---

[22]Based only on those constituencies which had such activities,
the Gamma correlations were .158 and .214 respectively.

Table II-B

The Relative Weight of Agriculture and Religion in 1844

Strongest Farm Areas*	Religious Rank	
Mahantongos	2	
Union	5	
West Penn	3	
Rush	6	
Wayne	1	
Barry	7	
East Brunswick	4	Gamma = .286
Moderate Farm Areas		
Orwigsburg	4	
West Brunswick	2	
Pine Grove Twp.	3	
Schuylkill Haven	7	
Schuylkill Twp.	5	
Tamaqua	6	
Porter	1	Gamma = .047
Weak Farm Areas		
Pine Grove Bo.	2	
Branch	4	
Blythe	5	
Manheims	1	
Minersville	7	
East Norwegian	3	
Pottsville	6	Gamma = .333

Partial Gamma = .206

*The constituencies are ranked by % Democratic in each group.

Both problems remain if one attempts to control for the farm
factor by dividing the constituencies into farm and non-farm areas, but
in any case as Table II-B shows the partial correlation between the
doctrinal orthodoxy and the Democracy declines, but remains strong.
One or two deviant areas stand out. East Brunswick and Porter did
have small mining interests which at this time amy have been important.
East Brunswick also had a sizable population of Reformed Dutch - not
Germans, but Holland Dutch. Within the context of Schuylkill County
this normally Democratic group,[23] which was native born, may well have
been assimilated into the Anglo-American element and have favored the
Whigs. Schuylkill Haven had an odd mixture of German Brethern and German
Episcopalians as well as sizable English Episcopalian minority. Such
Germans may well have been responding to ethnicity more than religion, or
we may simply err in assigning these German Episcopalians to the devotionalist category since they were "high church."[24] All in all the ethno-religious
factor remained one of the primary determinants of voting behavior in Schuylkill
County. German Lutherans were mostly farmers to whom the tariff question meant
little; and it was in the area of cultural politics that the Democrats captured
this self-sufficient, tradition bound people who sought above else to be left
to themselves.

---

[23]On the political perference of the Dutch Reformed element
elsewhere see: Benson, Concept, p. 185, and Formisano, Birth of Mass
Political Parties, p.

[24]See Sidney Ahlstrom, A Religious History of the American
People (New Haven, 1972), p. 519.

In among Welsh and English mining element there were also
appearing increasing numbers of Irish Catholics who, if they could vote,
were undoubtedly Democrats to the man.[25] In response to the rioting
in Philadelphia Bannan had shown sympathy for nativist principles which
were at the time growing in the county, and in 1845 the Whig coalition
split. While the Democrats held tightly to their German Lutheran voting
base, the Whigs were demoralized. Their turnout declined and the short
lived Native American Party syphoned off Whig voters in Mount Carbon,
Minersville and Pottsville. The Democrats swept the election gaining
approximately 65% of the vote.

Both major parties were vigorously pro-tariff in the election and
no national question arose to separate the local parties. Although it was
ignored by the Democrats, Bannan and the Whigs again emphasized sabbatarianism. The Miners' Journal aggressively asserted that the Democrats sanctioned
immorality by refusing to honor the Sabbath, but this reformist stance did
not keep the most vigorous nativists within party ranks. The main result of
the Native American outbreak was to force the Whigs toward an ever greater
emphasis on cultural politics. However, before the Whigs could respond to
this growing nativism the Democratic administration handed them as issue of
even greater potency within Schuylkill County.

The Democratic orientation of Schuylkill County appeared
assured by 1845; then a sudden and quite startling change of events

---

[25]On the Democratic preference of the Irish see: Benson,
Concept, p. 171; and William Shannon, The American Irish (New York,
1963), p. 47.

took place. The Whigs swept to victories in 1846, 1847 and 1848 before
control of the state and the county once again returned to the Democrats
in 1849. The issue which had created an electoral surge for the Whigs
in 1846 was the Walker Tariff, a low tariff passed by the Democratic
Polk Administration in direct defiance of promises made by the Pennsylvania
Democrats that Polk favored a continuation of protection as outlined in
the 1842 Whig Tariff Law. This tariff uproar caused the first significant
shift in the political behavior of Schuylkill County's voters in its history.
These changes in the late 1840's tended to reinforce ethno-religious differences between the parties by unifying the English and causing a rift to
appear among the Germans.

The Polk Administration sponsored the Walker Tariff which reduced
the rates previously imposed by the Whig Tariff of 1842 passed during the
Tyler Presidency. Only one Pennsylvania Democrat in Congress, David Wilmot,
supported the Walker Tariff or McKay Bill as it was sometimes termed.[26] The
ironic twist for Pennsylvania's pro-tariff Democrats was that their native
son, George Dallas, then serving as Vice-President, broke a tie vote in the
Senate which ultimately passed the McKay Bill into law. The situation was
further aggravated by the fact that the Democrats had posed James K. Polk
as a staunch friend of protection during the presidential campaign of
1844.[27] The Whig presses of the state,

---

[26]Snyder, Jacksonian Heritage, p. 194.

[27]Ibid., p. 196.

Table II-C

1846 Whig Vote in Ten Selected Constituencies
of Schuylkill County

	1844%	1845%*	1846%**
Coal Region			
Pottsville	61	49	68
E. Norwegian	59	52	72
Minersville	58	23	60
Mt. Carbon	56	38	66
Branch	44	33	74
Farm Areas			
Up. Mahantongo	10	4	13
Union	17	11	17
Lo. Mahantongo	20	20	25
West Penn	28	23	31
Barry	33	21	27

*In 1845 the Native Americans gained 38% in Mt. Carbon, 17% in Minersville
and 11% in Pottsville.
**In 1846 the only significant Native American vote was 7% in
Pottsville and 5% in Minersville.
***Elsewhere Mt. Carbon is tabulated with the Manheims.

Table II-D

Turnout in Ten Selected Constitutencies
of Schuylkill County

	1844	1845	1846
Coal Region			
Pottsville	1191	969	1044
E. Norwegian	360	186	272
Minersville	292	198	300
Mt. Carbon	41	40	53
Branch	292	150	189
Farm Areas			
Up. Mahantongo	219	139	61
Union	151	71	99
Lo. Mahantongo	197	125	111
West Penn	295	145	151
Barry	124	57	75

including the Miners' Journal, now gleefully divided the Democrats into
pro-tariff and anti-tariff camps. "Which is the Democratic party?"
Bannan snidely remarked, "Both cannot be."[28]

The election of 1846 in Pennsylvania proved utterly devastating
to the Democrats. Whigs won seventeen of twenty-four Congressional seats
and control of both houses of the state legislature.[29] The tariff issue
took stage center in the political circles of Schuylkill County and the
results were equally disastrous to the county Democrats. The local
Whigs benefitted from the electoral surge created by the protection
turmoil increasing their proportion of the vote by 18% and building
majorities throughout the county.[30]

Providentially for the Whigs, coal production had risen
twofold between 1842 and 1845 after it had remained stable between
1837 and 1842.[31] Bannan naturally credited the Tariff of 1842 for this
large increase and predicted a dire turnabout now that the Walker Bill

_____

[28]Ibid., p. 197; Miners' Journal, Pct. 3, 1846, p. 2.

[29]Mueller, Whig Party, p. 133.

[30]Cf. Campbell, "Surge and Decline", pp. 397-418.

[31]The actual county coal production was as follows:
        1837 - 540,000 tons
        1842 - 572,000 tons
        1845 - 1,132,000 tons.

was in force.[32] This situation could only compound the political

agony of the Democrats. Rallying behind a popular issue, the Whigs

in Schuylkill County carried every local office and swept to clear

majorities in every contested elction. They pledged their entire

local ticket directly to the principles of the Tariff of 1842.

Bannan labeled the McKay Bill a "free trade" abomination, and insisted

that the Whigs would always prefer the workshops of the United States

to those of Europe.[33]

Democrats responded to these pro-tariff blasts by frankly

apologizing for the actions of Polk, Dallas and their national brethren

and espousing "modification" of the Walker Bill as fellow Pennsylvanian

James Buchanan had suggested.[34] The county Democrats were obviously

forced to the unpopular side of a damaging issue through no fault of

their own. The Whigs could now quite logically claim to be the only

true friends of protection on both local and national levels.

The Democratic Emporium attempted to play down the protection

question and desperately sought other reasons for the dramatic 1846

turnabout. One of the alibis used by the frantic Democrats even involved

the weather. It had rained heavily in the county on election day.

---

[32]Miners' Journal, August 22, 1846, p. 2. Snyder, Jacksonian
Heritage, p. 197.

[33]Miners' Journal, August 22, 1846, p. 2. Only minor mention
was made of the Mexican Campaign though the paper did warmly applaud
the exploits of Zachary Taylor and Winfield Scott, two Whig heroes.

[34]Snyder, Jacksonian Heritage, p. 198; Philip S. Klein, President
James Buchanan (University Park, 1962), pp. 172-74.

The Emporium lamented:

> In the densely populated Boroughs in the region --
> strongholds of Federalism (Whiggism), where there is but
> a step or two to the election grounds the voters were
> nearly all out, whilst in the sparse county districts,
> where our party polls its strong vote, and where voters
> have to go three or four miles to vote, it will be per-
> ceived that our friends did not come out in consequence
> of the bad weather.[35]

Table II-D gives voter turnout in selected urban and rural districts
in 1844, 1845, and 1846 show that the Emporium's excuse had some basis
in fact. The coal regions increased greatly their turnout while that
in the strongly Democratic rural areas actually declined. The losses
were especially heavy in isolated Upper Mahantongo Township where voters
traveled up to seven miles to a polling place. However, the Whigs
also carried the county again in 1847 and 1848, years of pleasant
election day weather and the latter of which witnessed one of the
largest turnouts in the County's history.

The tariff issue was the main reason for the change of political fortunes. This critical issue obviously made Whigs of swing
voters and motivated previously apathetic Whigs to become more diligent.
Judging from the remarkable number of county Whig meetings in 1846,
the tariff question helped forge a more efficient Whig organization.
This was the first year in which Bannan did not loudly complain about
Whig apathy. The Walker Tariff thus hurt the county Democrats in two
vital ways: it damaged their popularity; and it stimulated the political
activities of their opponents.

---

[35]Emporium, October 10, 1846, p. 2.

The elections of 1847 and 1848 brought a continuation of Whig success in Schuylkill County. The tariff remained the crucial issue which kept the once powerful county Democrats on the defensive. However, other questions continued to exert appreciable potency in determining voting behavior. For example, a critical local issue in 1847 was the question of the removal of the county seat from farm oriented Orwigsburg to Pottsville located in the heart of the anthracite region. The Whigs favored such a move while the Democrats opposed it. Ultimately 3,551 (53%) of the county's 6,643 voters supported relocation. The transfer was duly completed by 1851 when Pottsville officially became the county seat. The Whigs had identified themselves with the numerically popular side of yet another crucial local issue. They apparently retained most of the voters who had switched to their party the previous year and swept to victories in 1847 similar to those in 1846.

The Whig tide flowed into 1848 when both their presidential and gubernatorial candidates won easily with Taylor garnering 57% of the Schuylkill County ballots. Bannan and the Whigs continued to concentrate largely on the tariff issue. The Walker Tariff was continually assailed in the _Miners' Journal_ as the "British Tariff of 1846."[36] Lewis Cass and the Democrats were referred to as the "Free Trade Starvation Ticket."[37] A succinct paragraph from the _Miners' Journal_

---

[36] _Miners' Journal_, October issues, 1848.

[37] _Ibid._, September 30, 1848, p. 2.

vividly exemplifies just how important the county Whigs thought the
tariff was:

> The great battle to be fought in the next
> Congress, in repealing the British Bill of
> 1846, and restoring the Protective Policy of
> the Country on a permanent basis, . . . will
> secure for the laborer a just reward for his
> toil. . .[38]

The county Whigs endeavored to convince the voters that only
through protection could the American worker achieve just economic rewards.
The strategy was successful in that it appealed to the marginal mining
region electorate not solidly committed to a specific party.

Bannan discussed other national issues relevant to the campaign
of 1848 though none even approximated the emphasis which he placed upon
the tariff. The Miners' Journal never mentioned the Free Soil movement
except to remind its readers that Van Buren had long been personally
associated with a low tariff policy. The Whigs of the county applauded
Taylor's restraint in the utilization of his veto power. They also
supported his proposal to distribute federal funds realized by sales of
public lands. The county party further approved of Taylor's opposition
to the extension of slavery and support of internal improvements.[39] Yet,
the amount of space that the Miners' Journal gave to these latter issues
indicated they were afterthoughts. The tariff was the bellwether issue
in forging a Whig victory and the astute Bannan knew this. Oddly,
Bannan rarely discussed

---

[38]Ibid., September 23, 1848, p. 2.

[39]Ibid.

them people of all economic strata responded negatively to the Democrats.
Bannan had attributed the Whig victory in 1846 to the tariff question.
He called that election a "tariff triumph,"[41] and obviously 1848 carried
these emotions into presidential politics. Taylor did extremely well in
Pennsylvania, because pro-tariff Democrats deserted their party.[42] However,
Bannan insisted that the demise of the independent nativist movement and its
merger with the Whigs also played a key role in the rout of the Democrats.[43]

Actually the shifts taking place in county voting patterns
were quite complicated. In percentage terms the Whigs gained practically
everywhere. Only on Porter and the Manheims was the trend reversed;
and even such staunch German constituencies as Barry and West Brunswick
moved into the Whig column. The relationship between wealth and party
preference continued to be modest and favor the Democrats. Religious
orientation became slightly more important as Bannan indicated, but the
most important difference between the parties was now an urban/rural
polorization. Boroughs such as Pine Grove, Tamaqua, Schuylkill Haven,
and Port Clinton turned in Whig majorities, and in the only remaining
Democratic borough, Orwigsburg the Democratic vote fell from 67% to 56%.
The correlation between farming and the Democracy rose to .740. The
Whigs were the beneficiaries of both nativism and the tariff in a way

---

[41] Miners' Journal, October 17, 1846, p. 2.

[42] Holman Hamilton, Zachary Taylor (Indianapolis, 1951), II, pp. 86-113.

[43] Miners' Journal, August, 29, 1846, p. 2. Bannan predicted this before the elction.

the character or charisma of Taylor. He, of course, referred to his
gallantry at Buena Vista and Palo Alto, but Taylor's tariff views
appealed far more to Bannan and his readers than his military exploits.

Several other factors are worth noting concerning the 1848
race in the county. First, Van Buren and the Free Soilers failed to
gain a single vote in Schuylkill County. This lack of Free Soil appeal
undoubtedly accounted for the sparcity of Bannan attacks upon Van Buren
and his fellow non-extensionists.[40] Secondly, the Whigs were appealing
to the Welsh and the English both religiously and economically since
they were largely devotionalists and involved with mining. For example,
Pottsville, Minersville and Port Carbon together gave Taylor 1,642 votes
to Cass' 669 for a majority of 973. There can be no doubt that the Whigs
were winning because they had increased their victory margins in areas
where they were already the majority party. Thirdly, the German Lutherans
did not respond as aggressively to the tariff issue as did the English
and Welsh. They and the growing Irish Catholic element were basically
motivated by religious and ethnic considerations. Consequently, the
Whigs had the advantage during the period when the tariff had created
an electoral surge situation.

The turnout in 1848 reached 80% of the white adult males and
was particularly strong in the mining areas. Obviously these districts
were most influenced by the Walker Tariff which lowered rates imposed on
competing British coal and iron products, and in

---

[40]Elsewhere in the state, German Lutherans were extremely
hostile to the Free Soil movement. See: Peterson, "Reaction to a
Heterogeneous Society," pp. 221-222. Most of the Free Soil vote came
from David Wilmot's normally Democratic Congressional district.

that was bound to produce an unstable coalition. Sweeping all before
it, the tariff mania brought many non-devotionalist English and the
urban Germans, whose economic interests were threatened, into the Whig
party at least momentarily. As the situation changed, these groups would
respond in contrasting fashions, but for a moment this coalition held
control of the county.

The years between 1849 and 1852 saw a return to power by the
Democrats in Schuylkill County. The Democratic coalition now appeared
to be centered solely around Irish Catholics and German Lutherans. No
longer could the Democrats depend upon their share of English Protestant
support. However, the continuing influx of Irish Catholics into the
region appeared to be compensating for these losses. The county's
population had skyrocketed 106% between 1840 and 1850, and Irish Catholics
represented a sizable portion of this increase. By the late 1850's,
the Irish Catholics comprised about 25% of the county's population.[44]
Nearly every Irish Catholic who received the franchise voted Democratic;
hence, it is easy to comprehend why the new Democratic coalition, even
though virtually devoid of devotionalistic support, was as powerful as
the Democratic machine which dominated the county prior to 1846.

The growing power of Irish Catholic votes in the county can
be easily demonstrated. The Democrats were generally

---

[44]See Table I-B for population figures. English and Welsh
miners also arrived between 1840 and 1860 but not in such numbers as
did the Irish Catholics. It must be remembered that Ireland was undergoing serious political and economic unrest during these years. As
the Irish, Welsh and English entered the county, its German proportions
naturally dropped in relation to the other ethnic groups.

Table II-E

1848 Ranking of Schuylkill Minor Civil Divisions
on Four Variables

	1 Party	2 Wealth	3 Religion	4 Agriculture
Union	1	15	6	1
West Penn	2	2	3	2
Rush	3	21	7	5
Mahantongoes	4	13	2	3
Wayne	5	6	1	4
Porter	6	20	5	9
Pine Grove Twp.	7	12	10	11
Orwigsburg	8	17	11	15
Barry	9	16	8	6
West Brunswick	10	19	9	8
Manheims	11	7	12	13
East Brunswick	12	14	4	7
Schuylkill Hav.	13	18	17	14
Tamaqua	14	1	15	10
Blythe	15	8	19	17
Pine Grove Bo.	16	10	14	12
E. Norwegian	17	3	16	19
Branch	18	9	18	18
Schuylkill Twp.	19	4	13	16
Minersville	20	5	21	21
Pottsville	21	11	20	20

$\text{Gamma}_{1 \cdot 2} = -.285$ $\text{Gamma}_{1 \cdot 3} = .657$ $\text{Gamma}_{1 \cdot 4} = .740$

Table II-F

Vote in Districts Incorporated Between 1848 and 1852

	% of Irish Catholics in District in 1850*	1852 %Democratic
Mahanoy	75 - 80	88
Cass	60 - 65	66
Butler	50 - 55	67
Frailey	45 - 50	59
Norwegian**	45 - 50	59
St. Clair	35 - 40	42

*Estimates based upon the figures given in 1850 and 1860 census reports.
**Returns reported separately after 1848.

and sometimes overwhelmingly being supported in the newly established
voting districts in the county. All of the districts which were
founded between 1848 and 1852 contained significant Irish Catholic
populations. Table II-F shows the proportions of votes given to the
Democrats in these areas.

Clearly, the voting pendulum in Schuylkill County had shifted to once again favor the Democrats. The emerging Irish Catholic vote
was largely responsible for the shift. Because of the allegiance of this
group the Democrats managed to increase their percentages in the established coal regions and gain heavy majorities in the newly formed mining
districts. By 1852 the Democrats had regained their former position in
the German Lutheran farm regions; and the German boroughs of Mount Carbon,
Port Clinton and Orwigsburg were once again solidly Democratic. Porter and
East Brunswick also shifted. Thus, the altered Democratic coalition pre-
pared for a long period of dominance in Schuylkill County.

Those areas which had switched to the Whigs in 1846 and still
remained in 1852 were characterized by large Welsh and English populations
and a devotionalist religious orientation (Table II-G). There was now a
significant correlation between wealth and Democratic voting. The farm
areas continued to be strongly Democratic, but the correlation

Table II-G

1852 Ranking of Schuylkill County Minor Civil Divisions on Four Variables

	1 Party	2 Wealth	3 Religion	4 Agriculture
Union	1	15	6	1
Rush	2	21	7	5
Mahantongos	3	13	2	3
Barry	4	16	8	6
Porter	5	20	5	9
Orwigsburg	6	17	11	15
West Penn	7	2	3	2
Wayne	8	6	1	4
Pine Grove Twp.	9	12	10	11
West Brunswick	10	19	9	8
Manheims	11	7	12	13
East Brunswick	12	14	4	7
Schuylkill Haven	13	18	17	14
Pine Grove Bo.	14	10	14	12
Blythe	15	8	19	17
Branch	16	9	18	18
Schuylkill Twp.	17	4	13	16
Tamaqua	18	1	15	10
Minersville	19	5	21	21
East Norwegian	20	3	16	19
Pottsville	21	11	20	20

$Gamma_{1.2} = -.440$ $Gamma_{1.3} = .600$ $Gamma_{1.4} = .691$

Table II-H

The Relative Weight of Agriculture and Religion in 1852

Religious Rank

Strongest Farm Areas*
Union	5
Rush	6
Mahantongos	2
Barry	7
West Penn	3
Wayne	1
East Brunswick	4

Gamma = −.238

Moderate Farm Areas
Porter	1
Pine Grove Twp.	3
West Brunswick	2
Manheims	4
Schuylkill Haven	7
Pine Grove Bo.	5
Tamaqua	6

Gamma = .715

Weak Farm Areas
Orwigsburg	1
Blythe	5
Branch	4
Schuylkill Twp.	2
Minersville	7
East Norwegian	3
Pottsville	6

Gamma = .333

Partial Gamma = .270

*All of these constituencies except Barry were 100% Lutheran and Reformed.

between devotionalism and Whig voting had grown in the mining areas.
The constituencies which were 100% German Lutheran ranged from 69% to
85% Democratic, while half or more of the churches in Whig areas were
devotionalist in orientation. The English and Welsh Protestants
overwhelmingly rejected the new Democratic coalition. In general,
the continuing German Lutheran support of the Democrats combined with
the growing Irish Catholic vote to assure Democratic supremacy in
Schuylkill County.

The Whig "style" of politics had become noticeably different
from that of the Democrats. The Whigs, as exemplified by Bannan, under-
took moralizing crusades not just campaigns. Politically, this meant
that the Whigs felt a deep concern for the social and moral well being
of their community. Their ultimate goal was to achieve a moral society
through the control of certain aspects of individual behavior. They were,
in a sense, "fanatical pietists" endeavoring to use government power to
rectify the evils of American society as they perceived them.[45] The Whigs
were as quick to support nativism, temperance and sabbatarianism as the
tariff.

The Democrats of the county lacked this revivalistic fervor.
They favored a more passive governmental structure in which there
would be a minimal interference with individual freedom. Lee Benson
has termed their general approach to the role of government, "negative
liberalism."[46] The government should ideally be laissez-faire in

---

[45] Jensen, "Religious and Occupational Roots of Party Identification," pp. 330-32.

[46] Benson, Concept, pp. 86-109.

style and tolerate all forms of political and religious behavior which were not detrimental to society. This meant that Democrats rejected governmental regulation of immigration, Sunday sales and alcoholic consumption as undue paternalism.

The county Democrats completely rejected the Whigs' support of temperance, sabbatarianism, nativism and anti-Catholicism. Instead, they pleaded causes more popular to their principal constituents. The Democratic press of the county, rather than condemning Irish Catholics, appealed to their sensitivities. For example, the local Democrats stood squarely against British landlords and for the Irish peasants in the domestic turmoil then plaguing Ireland:

> It is full time that, while the landlord
> is protected in his right to his property,
> the tenant should be protected from ex-
> tortion, spoilation and from expulsion
> from his farm.[47]

The local Democrats condemned statements by Whigs which asserted that "it would be a great blessing if every Whiskey Factory in the country could be closed up."[48] They viewed enforced temperance as an usurpation of individual liberty. Sabbatarianism came under similar fire from local Democrats.

In the 1852 election Bannan toned down his emphasis on moral reform and even made ovatures to the Irish Catholics pointing out nativist acts of Democrats and attacking the "lazy [English] tithemen in Ireland."[49] Basically the Whig editor focused upon the tariff in

---

[47]The Pottsville Register and Democrat, September 28, 1850, p. 2. (This paper will hereafter be cited as the Register.)

[48]Miners' Journal, June 8, 1850, p. 2.

[49]Miners' Journal, August 14, and October 9, 1852.

an unsuccessful attempt to hold together the victorious coalition of

1848. To Bannan:

> This campaign is plainly a struggle between
> protection and free trade--between a fostering
> of Home manufactures and the sustaining of
> remunerating prices of American labor, and
> the encouragement of Foreign manufactures
> and the introduction of the rates of European
> wages.[50]

But neither the major economic questions of the day nor

sectional issues differentiated Schuylkill County parties. The Democrats

also claimed to support a protective tariff and joined the Whigs in

opposing incorporation of the collieries. Both parties supported the

Compromise of 1850. The Democrats responded to Bannan by warning the

Irish not to be tricked by his tactics into supporting the moralizing

and basically anti-Catholic Whigs.[51] With booming times in the coal

fields,[52] the tariff issue lost much of its potency and voter turnout

declined. The county remained divided between the Democratic coalition

of German Lutheran farmers and Irish Catholic miners, and the urban, coal-

oriented English and Welsh Protestant Whigs. The Whigs could win only

when they posed solely as the protectors of the county's mining interest,

but to a suicidal extent they refused to limit themselves to economic

appeals and embraced cultural politics.

---

[50]Ibid., August 14, 1852. See also: Miners' Journal, June 19,
1852.

[51]Pottsville Mining Register, October 9, 1852.

[52]County coal output in tons was:

1848	1,733,721
1849	1,728,500
1850	1,840,620
1851	2,328,225
1852	2,637,835.

B. Democrats Versus Republicans, 1853-1872

As in the earlier period, the Democrats were the majority
party through most of this era. Their dominance was interrupted only
in the elections of 1858, 1859 and 1860 when the Democrats were weaken-
ed by an internal split involving the Kansas question and the pro-
Southern policies of the Buchanan Administration. Only when the Democrats
were not united and faced with critical issues to which their responses
were unpopular with local voters, were the Republicans able to garner
a plurality of the votes cast in the county. National issues combined
in the late 1850s to produce a Republican surge in popularity and a short
term deviation in electoral patterns before the reinstatement of Democratic
supremacy in 1861. However, the years between 1853 and 1872 presented
political patterns in Schuylkill County strikingly similar to those of
the previous decade although demographic change did alter the county's
political structure heightening the importance of ethno-religious
differences.

Between 1853 and 1857 the Democratic renaissance evident in the
election of 1852 continued unabated as Irish Catholic newcomers joined
the German Lutheran farmers to swell the party's majorities. At the
same time the county Whig organization was coming apart at the seams.
Actually the October elections in 1852 had been rather close because
of a proposal for the division of the county which caused some "lower
enders" to bolt the Democrats,[53] but the presidential election proved

---

[53] Miners' Journal, October 16, 1852; Mining Register,
October 9, 1852.

to be an unmitigated disaster for the Whigs. Pierce easily carried
the county; and Bannan admitted that his party had "been whipped all
thro."[54] The columns of the Miners' Journal revealed the open frus-
tration and disillusionment which had overtaken county Whigs. Bannan
directly blamed the Irish for the rout claiming that "7/8 of the
Catholic vote was cast for Pierce."[55]

Whig resentment was summed up in a Bannan editorial assertion
that it was senseless for the Whigs to ever expect Catholic support
and the editor's shift toward militant anti-Catholicism. All appeals
to the Irish had failed. "This depending on the Foreign Catholic Vote,"
Bannan groaned, "is like destroying our own market for produce and then
depending on foreign countries to take it."[56] It now appeared time to
form a party which openly condemned all vestages of Romanism. Increasingly Catholicism emerged as the evil force behind much that was wrong
within the county and the nation. Bannan called upon the Whigs to purge
Catholics from the party and even linked them to free trade asserting
that "the controlling power of the Catholic Church does not want protection
to American industry."[57]

The salient issues in 1853 all had distinct ethno-religious
overtones and county Whigs split badly on how to respond to them.

---

[54] Miners' Journal, November 6, 1852.

[55] Ibid.

[56] Miners' Journal, August 15, 1853.

[57] Ibid.

Although it remained the party organ, the Miners' Journal now believed that temperance was the paramount issue facing the county's voters and that Pennsylvania's "greatest single need" was a "Prohibitory Liquor Law."[58] The temperance movement in Pennsylvania had been growing since 1851 when Maine passed a prohibition bill. Leading Whigs like Bannan, Edward O. Parry, John Wren and George Jennings were central figures at county temperance meetings.[59] The Miners' Journal plainly took its stand on the issue:

> We are daily becoming more and more persuaded that nothing short of a prohibitory law can reach the root of the evil, or effectively cure this moral leprosy in Schuylkill County.[60]

The temperance question in Schuylkill County was solidly rooted in anti-Catholicism. Bannan often cited the tendency of "foreigners" to be involved in the dispensing as well as the consuming of spirits and decryed the social consequences of their behavior.[61] The Miners' Journal claimed that 191 of the county's 356 legal paupers were Irish Catholics and that most had been driven to their fate by intemperance.[62] Bannan also lamented the fact that the county's coal regions had 636 taverns -- one for every nine voters -- most of which were frequented primarily by Irish Catholics.[63]

---

[58] Miners' Journal, July 2, 1853.

[59] Miners' Journal, July 30, 1853.

[60] Miners' Journal, July 2, 1853.

[61] Miners' Journal, August 6, and October 1, 1853.

[62] Miners' Journal, June 25, 1853.

[63] Ibid.

Anti-Catholicism also served to relate temperance to other moral issues. Bannan and the Whigs had consistantly taken a sabbatarian position, and now the Miners' Journal added gross disrespect for the sabbath to the list of Irish Catholic sins.[64] As a long term advocate of common schools, Bannan was particularly disturbed by Catholic attempts to divide school funds in order to support parochial schools. He considered this the second most important question before the voters; and, in an attempt to cut into the German vote, he reminded them that a recent Lutheran synod had condemned Catholic efforts "to mutilate our common schools."[65]

Not all Whigs were as ardent in their support of these issues as Bannan. When the regular Whig organization hesitated to take a firm stand on sabbatarianism, temperance, and the school question, Bannan led a bolt that put forward an alternative Prohibition-Whig slate of candidates for the state assembly who were solid "Maine Law supporters" and supported restoring "good Puritan notions of the country."[66]

Nativism also had a minor impact upon the Democrats as a third opposition ticket, the Native Americans, entered the field; but their opponents were hopelessly fragmented and the Democratic candidates easily won. However, they did not receive a majority and Bannan saw in this the possibility for an anti-Catholic coalition built upon a merger of the Prohibition and American parties.[67]

---

[64] Miners' Journal, August 6, 1853.

[65] Miners' Journal, October 1, 1853.

[66] Miners' Journal, October 1, 1853.

[67] Miners' Journal, April 15, 1854.

Following the defeat of the prohibition bill in early 1854, the Miners'
Journal saw only one possible course of action for the "friends of
Temperance":

> to effect a thorough and complete organization, and
> enter the political field in a solid phalanx, as a
> separate party.[68]

Bannan called upon all Whigs to join this new organization but he made it
clear that the traditional Whig party was no longer adequate as the anti-
Democratic vehicle in the county.

The issues discussed in 1854 were similar to those of 1853.
Temperance, Catholic influences within the public schools and the
general evils of "popery" were often found dominating the pages of the
Miners' Journal. The attack on local Irish Catholics, however, grew
more intense in 1854. The Miners' Journal again dedicated columns to
showing that Irish Catholics were crowding county jails and pauper
institutions. The journal noted that 155 of the 282 people committed
to county institutions in 1853 were Irish Catholic as were 97 of about
200 county supported paupers.[69]

The results of local elections in 1854 proved how deeply the
temperance issue had eroded Whig strength. In the races for state
assembly, the Whigs ran one candidate of their own and endorsed another
who also had Prohibitionist support. The candidate running simply as
a Whig received only 359 votes while the Whig-Prohibitionist endorsement
polled 4,436 votes.[70] (Both assembly seats from the county, however,
were won by Democrats.) In the gubernatorial race James Pollock, an

---

[68] Miners' Journal, April 8, 1854.

[69] Miners' Journal, September 30, 1854.

[70] Miners' Journal, October 14, 1854.

ex-Whig supporter of nativism and prohibition, garnered 4,252 votes though he trailed Democrat William Bigler by over 1,000 votes in the area.[71]

It is worth noting that no strong editorial reference to the Kansas-Nebraska Act appeared in the 1854 editions of the Miners' Journal. The issues related to this bill were obviously not politically powerful in the county. The final collapse of county Whiggery seemed to occur when the rejection of a state prohibitory law made it obvious to temperance men that only an independent party, unequivocably committed to prohibition, could achieve the passage of an anti-liquor statute.

The years between 1855 and 1857 saw the Democrats become more powerful than ever in the county. They swept all local races and generally amassed between 55% and 60% of the vote in each contest. The floundering anti-Democratic coalition could rely on majorities during the mid-1850's only in Pottsville. These poor showings resulted mainly from the lack of unity among opponents of the county Democrats. This situation changed slightly in 1856 when they adopted the title the People's Party and frankly admitted its close ties with the national Republican organization.[72] The "Creed" of this new party was quite clear. It stood for non-extension, a high protective tariff, internal improvements as the expense of the federal government and restriction of Catholics.[73]

---

[71] Ibid.

[72] At times, the People's Party referred to itself as the Union Party especially late in the 1850's.

[73] Miners' Journal, Nov. 15, 1858, p. 2.

The last of these positions wielded more influence than any of the others
upon the politics of the county. Both anti-Catholicism and non-extension
served to sharply differentiate the People's Party from their Democratic
rivals, but it was the former that far and away received the greatest
attention in Schuylkill County.

Religious questions were of extreme importance in the county
since the Democrats were markedly anti-Negro and gave considerable
attention to the argument that the free Negro represented a direct
economic threat to the common white laborer of the North. The Miners'
Journal, still the foremost anti-Democratic paper of the county, stated
explicitly that the People's Party opposed Catholics and parties which
courted the Catholic voters. It continued to call for a prohibition
law and even suggested that violators of such a law be "punished like
murderers."[74] The Miners' Journal went to great lengths to assure voters
that the People's Party's candidates were English and Welsh, friends
of protection and foes of Catholicism.[75]

Virtually every issue discussed during these years had distinct
religious overtones. In a sweeping editorial, Bannan asserted that the
Irish Catholics contributed to every socially malady then existing in
American society. He accused the Irish Catholics of receiving fraudulent
naturalization papers, cheating honest voters by "colonizing" election
districts, holding allegiances to "foreign potentates" and leading the

[74] Miners' Journal, July 11, 1857, p. 3.

[75] Miners' Journal, October 1, 1856, p. 2.

illicit and violent "Molly Maguire Associations."[76]

As Table II-I shows while wealth remained unimportant however, the county was no longer politically divided into Democratic farm areas and Peoples' mining areas and religious differences had come to be even more acute than they had been in 1852. Although this may not be apparent at first because of the decline in the correlation coefficient, there is less "static" caused by the farm/mine split and the problems of missing data all work to suppress this relationship. In 1856 mining areas, Cass, Norweigen, New Castle, Butler and Blythe were among the top half of the constituencies in Democratic vote yet the large number of Irish Catholics in these areas are not reflected in the 1850 data. The new People's Party clearly advocated programs which appealed to devotionalists while alienating the more doctrinally orthodox. The cleavage was obvious and the voters cast their ballots in an equally distinct fashion. One portent of the future was the shift toward the new party in several traditionally German areas. North Manheim, Barry, Eldred, Pine Grove Borough and Porter remained Democratic, but they had earlier responded to the American party, and eventually would become Republican.

---

[76] Ibid., Oct. 10, 1857, p. 2. This may have been the first mention of the Molly Maguires in the county. The Molly Maguires were allegedly an Irish Catholic secret society which took violent actions against the foes of these Irish Catholics. They were generally viewed as the violent wing of the fraternal organization called the Ancient Order of Hibernians. For detailed studies of the Mollies and their environment see: Walter J. Coleman, The Molly Maguire Riots: Industrial Conflict in the Pennsylvania Coal Region (New York, 1936); Wayne Broehl, Jr., The Molly Maguires (Cambridge, 1964); Arthur H. Lewis, Lament for the Molly Maguires (New York, 1969); Harold W. Aurand, From the Molly Maguires to the United Mine Workers: The Social Ecology of an Industrial Union, 1869-1897 (Philadelphia, 1972); Anthony J. Anspach, "The Molly Maguires in the Anthracite Coal Regions of 1850-1890; Being an Inquiry into Their Origin, Growth and Character and a Study of Absentee Ownership of the Coal Fields," Now & Then, Vol. XI, (Oct., 1954) pp. 25-34; Victor R. Greene, "The Molly Maguire Conspiracy in the Pa. Anthracite Region, 18621862-1879," unpublished M.A. Thesis, University of Rochester, 1960.

Table II-I

1856 Ranking of Schuylkill County Minor Civil Divisions on Three Variables

	1 Party	2 Wealth	3 Religion
West Penn	1	2	3
Rush	2	25	8
Union	3	16	7
Orwigsburg	4	18	12
Mahantongos	5	14	2
East Brunswick	6	15	5
West Brunswick	7	22	11
Pine Grove Twp.	8	13	4
Blythe	9	9	22
Wayne	10	6	1
New Castle	11	7	25
Butler	12	24	9
Manheims	13	8	13
Porter	14	23	6
Barry	15	17	10
Tremont	16	21	17
Tamaqua	17	1	18
Schuylkill Twp.	18	4	14
Schuylkill Haven	19	19	20
Branch	20	10	21
East Norwegian	21	3	19
Frailey	22	20	15
Minersville	23	5	24
Pottsville	24	12	23
Pine Grove Bo.	25	11	16

$Gamma_{1.2} = -.013$ $Gamma_{1.3} = .487$

By 1857 the local parties had not moved far beyond the positions which had earlier characterized Whigs and Democrats. The People's coalition was more intensely and overtly anti-Catholic than the old Whig Party, but it generally appealed to the same ethno-religious groups. The local Democrats took up anti-Negro positions, but remained the friends of the Catholics and refused to give support to strict naturalization laws or prohibition proposals. But the situation was in a state of flux. The returns in 1856 only correlated modestly with those of 1852 (r_s=.77). The Whig party had been thoroughly disrupted by the nativist and temperance questions in 1853, and the Irish presence was increasingly apparent among the Democrats.

The opponents of the Democrats again needed an electoral surge which could give them a chance at victory. The conditions for such a deviation from the county norm materialized in 1858. This electoral surge which gave the Republicans a three year reign of power in the county was related to the Buchanan administration's failure to deal adequately with key sectional disputes and the onset of the Civil War. Specifically, the 1858 demise of the Democrats in Schuylkill County could be attributed to Buchanan's handling of the volatile situation in Kansas and his support of the Tariff of 1857 which lowered rates back to the levels of the only mildly protective tariff of 1816. President Buchanan, a Pennsylvanian, took a pro-Southern stance on both Kansas and the tariff. The unpopularity of Buchanan's position, especially in reference to Kansas, was so pronounced that it caused a split in the local Democratic organization.

As in the late 1840's, national Democratic low tariff programs could only damage the county Democrats who were located in an area which was highly sensitive to the issue. The impact of all these issues plus the split in the Democratic ranks led to the first Democratic losses since 1848 in Schuylkill County.

The People's Party made their biggest 1858 gains in the coal regions of the county particularly those in which mines were recently opened. Table II-J indicates that the Democrats had lost considerable support in the coal districts since their strong showings in 1856. The people in this area reacted negatively to the pro-Southern tariff policies of the Buchanan administration.

Voters in traditional Democratic areas also showed a tendency to turn away from the Democrats, but they were obviously less concerned by the issues of 1858. Buchanan had done nothing to directly anger either the Irish Catholics or the German Lutherans, and in general retained their traditional loyalty. Table II-K indicates that the 1856 Democratic strongholds wavered little in their voting habits. They still gave the Democrats overwhelming majorities though all districts did show a slight decline in Democratic percentages.

The decline of the Democrats can be traced directly to gains registered by the People's Party in the coal districts of the county. However, significant gains were also being scored by the People's Party among the urban Germans of the county. Boroughs like Schuylkill Haven, Cressona, Orwigsburg, Pine Grove and Auburn were no longer following the traditional Democratic tendencies of their fellow Germans in the rural

Table II-J

People's Party Vote in Five Coal Region Districts

1856, 1858

	1856%	1858%
Branch	53	71
St. Clair	50	59
Pottsville	57	63
Tamaqua	49	56
Minersville	58	63

Table II-K

Democratic Strongholds 1856, 1858

	1856%	1858%
Cass	88	73
Upper Mahantongo	87	81
West Brunswick	86	75
Union	81	78
Washington	81	69
West Penn	73	71

*The 1858 total includes the combined percentages of Lecompton and anti-Lecompton Democrats.

Table II-L

Vote in Urban, German Districts in 1858

	Democrat %
Orwigsburg	57
Schuylkill Haven	43
Pine Grove Borough	29
Cressona	27
Auburn	18

townships. Table II-L shows just how much less Democratically oriented these urban German areas were than the county's rural German districts. The Democrats did not gain a majority in any of these districts and in Auburn garnered on 18% of the total vote.

The crucial election of 1858 caused a realignment in the politics of the county. The Democrats were still the German Lutheran-Irish Catholic coalition, but their opponents were now a coalition of Welsh and English Protestants and urban Germans who lived in five key commercial boroughs located in the farm sectors of the county. These urban Germans were apparently less isolated, less residentially homogeneous and more responsive to the issues of 1858 than were their rural counterparts.[77]

The voting behavior of the Germans in Schuylkill County indicates that many factors influenced their party choice. Included among these determinants apparently were economic role, place of residence, degree of isolation and amount of residential heterogeneity. The Germans of the boroughs were also less heavily Lutheran than their rural brethren. For example, German Wesleyan sects were found in four of these boroughs while the rural German areas generally contained only Lutheran or Reformed churches.

---

[77] Not all Germans voted alike in the Civil War era, see: Formisano, Mass Political Parties, pp. 298-305; Andreas Doraplen, "The German Element and the Issues of the Civil War," Mississippi Valley Historical Review, XXIX (June, 1942), pp. 55-76; Paul Kleppner, "Lincoln and the Immigrant Vote: A Case of Religious Polarization," Mid-America, XLVIII (July, 1966), pp. 176-195; George H. Daniels, "The Immigrant Vote in the 1860 Election: The Case of Iowa," Mid-America, XLIV (July, 1963), pp. 142-162; Joseph Schafer, "Who Elected Lincoln," American Historical Review, XLVIII (Oct. 1951), pp. 51-63. Also see Kleppner, Cross of Culture, pp. 79-83 for a thorough discussion of German voting behavior during the period.

If the German Protestants in the farm oriented boroughs
were swinging away from the Democrats, it can be assumed that the
non-Lutheran German Protestants living in the coal boroughs were at
least partially responsible for the shifts away from the Democrats in
those areas. The degree of assimulation into the Anglo-American
culture, the religious style and the economic orientation of large
numbers of the county's Germans was changing (Table II-M). The People's
coalition was then more formidable than the old Whig alliance since it
could count on a good deal more German support.

The 1858 Democratic demise must be attributed partly to the
Lecompton split in the county party. In the six major local races in
1858, two slates of Democratic candidates were advanced, the Lecomptonites and anti-Lecomptonites. The combined Democratic vote exceeded the
People's vote in two of these contests. Hence, the split at least
assured the People's Party of an electoral sweep of the county. The
Democratic schism made all six elections landslides.

The Lecompton split in the county Democratic organization
turned the major elements of the Democratic coalition against each
other. The strongest anti-Lecompton areas were the German Lutheran
areas (Table II-N). The "regular" Democrats outnumbered the anti-
Lecomptonites in the mining districts of the county.[78] The anti-
Lecomptonites actually received better than half of the total vote
in some German Lutheran areas. Assuming that most coal region Democrats

---

[78] Overall, the Lecompton or regular Democrats received 26-29%
of the county vote while the anti-Lecomptonites polled 20-23%, depending on which race one counts.

Table II-M

Major Churches of Schuylkill County, 1850-1870*

	1850	1860	1870
Lutheran	30	36	24
German Reformed	4	19	26
Methodist	18	44	18
Presbyterian	9	4	6
Roman Catholic	6	15	18
Baptist	5	11	14
Episcopal	5	9	7
Evangelical Association	-	-	10

*Based upon the number of churches in the county's leading denominations given in the 1850, 1860 and 1870 United States published census returns.

Table II-N

Lecompton and anti-Lecompton Percentages
in Selected German Lutheran Areas

	Lecompton %	anti-Lecompton %
Washington	58	10
West Penn	54	14
Wayne	24	24
West Brunswick	21	50
Union	19	58
Upper Mahantongo	13	68

were Irish Catholics who were Lecomptonites, a potentially dangerous rift then began to appear in the Democratic coalition.

In contrast to this anti-Lecompton strength in German Lutheran areas, the regular Democrats fared relatively well in the Irish Catholic areas. For example, the regulars ran well ahead of the anti-Lecomptonites in Cass Township and had solid majorities in other Irish Catholic centers such as New Castle and Norweigen. The regulars managed to outpoll the anti-Lecomptonites in most of the coal regions, areas where a large percentage of the Democrats were Irish Catholics.

Hence, the voting patterns of the election of 1858 are easily definable in ethno-religious terms. The German Protestants who lived in the county's urban areas were joining the anti-Democratic coalition along with the Welsh and English Protestants, the traditional foes of the Democrats. But the issues of the day worked against the Democrats everywhere and this allowed the People's Party to take temporary control of the political events in the county. Irish Catholics and German Lutherans were still Democrats; however, the German Lutherans were markedly more anti-Southern than were their Irish Catholic allies.

The artful Bannan adroitly emphasized the issues of 1858 in the Miners' Journal. He linked the pro-Southernism of the Buchanan administration with the economic plight of the country concluding that Buchanan's desire to placate the South led to the disastrous tariff program of 1857.[79] Bannan constantly reminded his readers that the People's Party stood for "Freedom and Protection."[80] The anti-Catholic

---

[79] Miners' Journal, Sept. 18, 1858, p. 2.

[80] Ibid., August 28, 1858, p. 2.

crusade also continued in the _Miners' Journal_ which applauded loudly
when the county convention of the People's Party vowed to work for an
exclusion of all foreign labor.[81] Hence, Bannan was successfully link-
ing anti-Southernism, anti-Catholicism and protection proposals into
a broad program which had wide appeal in the county.

The People's Party continued on its successful path in 1859
despite the outward reunification of the local Democrats. However, the
new anti-Democratic coalition reached the height of its political power
in 1860 when it swept all races in the region by unprecedented margins.
In that year the People's coalition openly termed itself the Republican
Party and campaigned strenuously for the election of Abraham Lincoln.
The efforts of the local Republicans paid worthwhile dividends when
Lincoln received better than 57% of the votes in the November presidential
contest. The local Republican candidates had garnered similar margins
in the October contests.

Lincoln's overwhelming victory, which exceeded the close victory
of the ex-Know Nothing Andrew Curtin, obviously owed a great deal to his
reputation as a tariff advocate. Popular in all areas of the county,
Lincoln failed to excite the interest that had brought a negative vote
out against Curtin. Some German Lutherans must have gone for Lincoln and
others declined to vote while marginal voters in the coal regions gave
Lincoln their votes. Wealth and the proportion of foreign born had little
effect upon voting (Table II-O). The importance of occupation was declining as was that of religious style, but both remained strong. By

---

[81] _Ibid._, Sept. 4, 1858, p. 2.

Table II-O

1860 Ranking of Schuylkill County Minor Civil Divisions on Four Variables*

	1 Party	2 Wealth	3 Religion	4 Foreign Born
Union	1	27	3	20
Mahantongos	2	24	4	28
West Penn	3	25	5	29
Cass	4	4	17	3
East Brunswick	5	14	1	22
Manheims	6	13	10	18
Mahanoy	7	6	18	1
Wayne	8	18	2	26
New Castle	9	9	29	5
Rush	10	3	9	7
Schuylkill Twp.	11	28	7	11
West Brunswick	12	26	11	21
Pine Grove Twp.	13	8	6	25
Orwigsburg	14	21	8	24
Tamaqua	15	5	16	12
Eldred	16	19	19	27
Barry	17	15	12	13
Schuylkill Haven	18	7	14	19
Frailey	19	29	27	15
Minersville	20	2	20	10
St. Clair	21	1	28	2
Porter	22	16	24	17
Blythe	23	22	22	9
Pottsville	24	11	23	16
Butler	25	6	15	6
Tremont	26	10	13	14
Pine Grove Bo.	27	20	25	23
East Norwegian	28	12	21	4
Branch	29	23	26	8

$Gamma_{1.2} = -.098$ $Gamma_{1.3} = .497$ $Gamma_{1.4} = -.139$

*The four variables used here are: Party--a ranking of constituencies from the highest to the lowest in percent Democratic from Appendix A; Wealth--a ranking from the highest to the lowest per capita "Value of Real Estate" in 1868 from the Miners' Journal, December 12, 1868; Religion--a ranking of constituencies from highest to lowest on a scale of "doctrinal orthodoxy" based upon the manuscript 1850 United States Census for Pennsylvania supplimented by material from Munsell, History; Foreign Born--a ranking of constituencies from highest to lowest percent foreign born in 1870 from Table I-D.

moderating their emphasis on moralistic reform and emphasizing the economic interests of the county within the context of anti-Southernism, the Republicans were able to sweep the county picking up maj rities not only in the coal regions, but also such farm areas as Pine Grove Township, East Brunswick, and Orwigsburg. Lincoln received his strongest support from the traditional anti-Democratic areas of the county, the Welsh and English sectors of the coal regions. He also continued to receive the support of the urban Germans who had been swinging toward the Republicans since the mid 1850's. Although Lincoln may have gained a portion of the German Lutheran vote, he was unable to make any headway in the Irish Catholic districts.

The importance of the coal regions to Lincoln's victory cannot be lightly dismissed. Lincoln garnered 1,912 of his 2,039 vote majority in this area and swept several constituencies by over 70% (Table II-P). The Republicans carried every sizable mining district in the county with the exception of heavily Irish Catholic Cass Township where the Democrats received nearly 60% of the vote.

Table II-Q indicates that Lincoln also acquired strong support from German boroughs. For example, his lowest total in five such towns was the solid 55% which Orwigsburg afforded him. Obviously, these urban Germans were moving steadily away from their former Democratic propensities. By 1860, the Democrats could no longer count on a nearly even split in these areas. The assimulated, commercially oriented, evangelical Germans were fast becoming as anti-Democratic as the Welsh and English Protestants who generally resided in the county's coal regions.

Table II-P

Lincoln's Vote in the Coal Regions, 1860

	Lincoln %
Tremont	77
Butler	76
St. Clair	67
Minersville	66
Pottsville	70
Blythe	61
Branch	63
Tamaqua	52
Cass	43

Table II-Q

Lincoln's Vote in the Urban, German Areas, 1860

	Lincoln %
Auburn	79
Pine Grove Borough	77
Gressona	76
Schuylkill Haven	63
Orwigsburg	60

Table II-R

Lincoln Vote in German Lutheran Areas, 1860

	Lincoln %
Wayne	52
West Brunswick	40
Washington	35
West Penn	37
Upper Mahantongo	30
Union	21

Lincoln and his allies did not do well in the German Lutheran farm areas in 1860, although they cut into the usual Democratic majorities in these districts (Table II R). For the most part Schuylkill County's German Lutheran farmers refused to abandon their traditional Democratic leanings. These were the isolated, residentially homogeneous Germans of the county. Paul Kleppner termed Lutherans of this type in the Midwest "old style" Germans who most despised devotionalistic programs such as temperance, nativism and sabbatarianism.[82] There is no doubt that in Schuylkill County the Lutheran, rural Germans stood much more firmly behind their Democratic antecedents than did their urban counterparts. Yet, with each year they made up a shrinking proportion of the county's Germans.

Lincoln was elected by Welsh, English and urban German votes in Schuylkill County. His cause was aided by the sectional and tariff bunglings of the Buchanan administration. The anti-Southern attitudes undoubtedly intensified in the county by 1860 owing to the secession threats by some Southern states. Hence, two potent questions were working in his favor. Lincoln's position on the tariff was also certain and he was not a Know-Nothing. These factors all aided his cause immensely in the county.[83]

---

[82] Kleppner, Cross of Culture, p. 78.

[83] Most Pennsylvania Republicans favored Lincoln over Seward because of his protectionist leanings. One reason Lincoln was ultimately nominated was because of Pennsylvania's support. See, Reinhard Luthin. "Pennsylvania and Lincoln's Rise to the Presidency," Pennsylvania Magazine of History and Biography, LXVII (January, 1943), pp. 61-82, for a discussion of Lincoln's tariff views and his power in the Keystone State. See also: Luthin, The First Lincoln Campaign (Cambridge, Mass., 1944).

The locally discussed issues in 1860 reflected both the critical national problems of the day and long established local questions. The Republicans condemned Buchanan's pro-Southern policies and the threats of secession. Bannan also, quite naturally, lauded Lincoln and his high tariff position. The now Republican editor constantly referred to Lincoln as an "ex-Whig" who was a "tariff man to the core."[84] In an attempt to break the German vote the Republicans brought Carl Schurz into the county to speak in their favor. Anti-Catholicism had by no means disappeared as a local issue in 1860, but it was subsumed within the context of the quest for honest elections. The local Republicans formed "Wide Awake Clubs" to police election sites and curtail voting irregularities by Irish Catholics.[85]

The Republicans then reached the pinnacle of their strength in the county in 1860 when all major issues seemed to work in their favor. However, this situation quickly reversed itself in 1861 and the Democrats returned to power. Consequently, the Republicans controlled the county for only three brief years thanks to the inadequacies of Buchanan's policies and the anti-Southern feelings generated by the 1860 threats of secession. That these short term pre-Civil War issues no longer worked so heavily against the Democrats enabled them to return to their former position of dominance.

---

[84] Miners' Journal, June 2, 1860, p. 2.

[85] Ibid., Sept. 15, 1860, p. 21. Bannan had been complaining about Irish voting irregularities for years (see: Miner's Journal, October 3, 1857).

The resurgence of the Democrats can be attributed to many things. Most important among these was the fact that the county re-acted quite negatively to the early stages of the Civil War. The Democratic Standard of Pottsville was especially outspoken in its criticism of the conscription laws which favored the wealthier elements of society. The Democrats also claimed the war was becoming an abolitionist crusade and not merely an effort to thwart secession.[86] Such feelings, particularly among the Irish, were fired by racist Copperhead propaganda that led inevitably to resistence to the draft and the violent riots in Cass in 1862.[87] Thus, the Republicans suddenly found themselves on the negative side of issues related to the Civil War.

Another reason for the demise of Republican popularity was the drop in voter turnout. Only 12,159 votes were cast in 1861 compared to just over 14,000 in the gubernatorial election of 1860. Almost all of this drop was recorded in the coal regions. This meant that marginal, coal region voters were no longer motivated and failed to vote. The Morrill Tariff of March 1861 and war prosperity removed the economic motivation to support the Republicans.

Tables II S and II T indicate that the Republicans suffered substantial losses in the coal regions in 1861 while continuing to lose heavily in the German Lutheran areas. Deprived of heavy coal region majorities, the Republicans were forced to abandon political control in the county.

---

[86] Pottsville Democratic Standard, Aug. 31, 1861, p. 2. See also: Miners' Journal, August 9, 1862.

[87] It couldn't have helped that Bannan was the county's draft commissioner but he seems to have tried to keep conflict to a minimum (Alexander K. McClure, Old Time Notes of Pennsylvania [Philadelphia, 1905], I pp. 548-49).

Table II-S

Republican Vote in Coal Districts, 1860-1861

	1860%	1861%
Tremont	77	45
Butler	76	51
Blythe	61	37
St. Clair	67	46
Cass	39	25
Tamaqua	52	39
Branch	61	52
Minersville	66	57
Pottsville	64	55

Table II-T

Republican Vote in German Lutheran Districts, 1860 - 1861

	1860%	1861%
East Brunswick	44	34
West Brunswick	39	20
Washington	32	29
West Penn	32	31
Upper Mahantongo	31	27
Union	24	16

The decline in the potency of the tariff and anti-Southernism, the rise in the unpopularity of conscription and the Civil War, the fall off of voter interest in the coal regions and ongoing increase in Irish Catholic voters all combined to return the Democrats to power in 1861. The Republicans had lost the advantage they had gained just prior to the Civil War. However, the urban German support they had recently acquired represented the first time significant numbers of Germans had consistently supported a party other than the Democrats, and signaled the ultimate destruction of the mid-nineteenth century Democratic coalition.

The years between 1862 and 1872 saw the Democrats retain power in generally close elections. Religious issues took the central position in political conflict during these years especially after the close of the Civil War. The Irish Catholics came under particularly heavy fire from Bannan and the Miners' Journal throughout this decade. In 1862, the now dedicated Republican editor asserted:

> In Cass Township there has been a reign
> of terror for weeks. Many Protestants
> have been driven from their homes in
> that township lately under the threats
> of extreme violence.[88]

The Republicans also constantly saw more voters than people in Irish Catholic districts. They claimed that Cass Township had a voting list higher than its assessment list warranted.[89] Bannan openly blamed Sheriff Horan, an Irish Catholic, for permitting such violations in

---

[88] Miners' Journal, Oct. 18, 1862, p. 2.

[89] Ibid., Oct. 13, 1866, p. 2.

Cass and elsewhere. Obviously, the Republicans were acutely aware of

how powerful the Irish Catholic vote was becoming.

National issues continued to receive some attention during

this period. The Democrats tended to be critical of Lincoln's war

policies particularly anything which smacked of abolitionist influence

and in the post-war period opposed Republican Reconstruction policy.

In contrast, the county's Republicans attacked obstructionist Copper-

heads and took a strong radical stance. They gave unqualified en-

dorsement to Military Reconstruction and Black suffrage favored adoption

of the Fourteenth and Fifteenth Amendments, condemned race riots and

the Ku Klux Klan, supported Grant over Greeley in 1872, and ultimately

sided with Simon Cameron in his Pennsylvania power struggle with Andrew

Curtin.[90]

The Republicans also continued to concentrate on the tariff

issue as they had in the late 1850s. However, even the tariff question

was linked to religion since Bannan accused the "fenians" of the county

of being low tariff advocates.

> No one but an insane man expects the country
> to prosper without adequate protection to
> American Industry. Protection secures good
> wages against the competition of the low labor
> of Europe and is the working classes' security
> against the oppression of their employers.
> Only Fenians dispute this and support low
> tariffs and England.[91]

---

[90] Miners' Journal, October 14, 1865, August 18, 1866, typify
their position which seems to support Cox and Cox, "Negro Suffrage and
Republican Politics" and cast doubt upon the interpretation in Gillette,
The Right to Vote. On the Pennsylvania split see: Bradley, Triumph of
Militant Republicanism, pp. 179-221.

[91] Miners' Journal, October 13, 1866, p. 2.

The election of 1868 typified this period with Schuylkill
County giving its votes to the Democratic candidate Horatio Seymour
in a narrow victory. Bannan once again pushed tariff protection and
condemned the "Copperhead platform" as one of "Rebellion and Repudiation."[92]
Although a long time advocate of a paper currency to aid those "who created
wealth" against the power of paricite capitalists, the Republican editor
would have nothing to do with the Pendleton Plan which he viewed as "gross
hypocracy."[93] Chiding Democratic appeals to racism, the Miners' Journal
supported "Union and Liberty" and pledged themselves to the "safety of
men of all races."[94]

A local economic issue of county taxes did intrude into the
election. Since the Democrats were threatening to raise taxes, the
Republicans opposed any hike as unnecessary except to pad the coffers
of the local Irish dominated Democratic machine.[95] Bannan worked this
into his favorite issue - the political corruption of the Democrats based
upon the votes of unnaturalized Irish Catholics. He gave an anti-Catholic
twist to nearly every matter he discussed repeating his standard charges
against Irish paupers and the evil effects of "rum sellers."[96]

---

[92] Miners' Journal, August 29, September 19, 1868.

[93] David Montgomery, Beyond Equality (New York, 1967), p. 345;
Miners' Journal, August 29, October 3, 1868.

[94] Miners' Journal, October 10, November 7 and November 14, 1868.
Since Bannan often equated the Molly Maguires with the Ku Klux Klan this
statement had a double meaning relating to local violence as well as
that in the South.

[95] Miners' Journal, August 29, September 19, and October 10, 1868.

[96] Miners' Journal, August 15, 22, October 3, 10, and Nov. 14,
1868.

In 1868 voting patterns showed some differences from those
of 1860 and from the previous era (II-U). While the Irish townships
were extremely poor, so were several of the Welsh enclaves in the coal
regions; and the relationship between the wealth of a constituency and
its political behavior remained relatively inconsequential. The importance of occupation, however, had changed greatly (Table II-V). The
Republicans were far more successful in the farm districts than the Whigs
had ever been, and the emergence of the Irish had added a number of Irish
Catholic strongholds in the coal regions to the banner areas of the
Democracy. Immigration itself had little effect upon the political
patterns of the county. As in the earlier period, one could hardly
speak of a unified immigrant vote. Bannan appealed particularly to
English and Welsh immigrants to go through the naturalization process.
In 1868 he believed that there were one thousand such men in the county;
and he was confident that they would join their countrymen in Republican
ranks.[97] Yet, the relation between party preference and religious style
was more pronounced than ever and significant even in the top eleven farm
areas.[98] The post-war Republicans to a greater degree than any of their
predecessors were the party of dévotionalist Protestants while adherents
of doctrinal orthodoxy clustered in Democratic ranks.[99]

---

[97] _Miners' Journal_, August 22, 1868.

[98] This relationship is actually underrated in Table II-U, because areas such as Cass, Butler, Rush and most particularly New Castle
had a far larger Irish Catholic element than indicated here.

[99] _Ninth United States Census...1870_ (Washington, 1871), lists
the eleven farm districts in the county with an output of $100,000 in
value. For these districts the Gamma correlation between Democratic rank
and per/capita output is .180 and that between Democratic rank and
"doctrinal orthodoxy" is .562.

Table II-U

1868 Ranking of Schuylkill County Minor Civil Divisions on Four Variables

	1 Party	2 Wealth	3 Religion	4 Foreign Born
Mahantongos	1	24	4	28
Union	2	27	3	20
West Penn	3	25	5	29
Cass	4	4	17	3
Butler	5	11	15	6
Rush	6	3	9	7
East Brunswick	7	14	1	22
Wayne	8	18	2	26
Pine Grove Twp.	9	8	6	25
Schuylkill Twp.	10	28	7	11
West Brunswick	11	26	11	21
New Castle	12	9	29	5
Tremont	13	10	13	14
Tamaqua	14	5	16	12
Mahanoy	15	6	18	1
Manheims	16	13	10	18
Orwigsburg	17	21	8	24
Barry	18	15	12	13
Schuylkill Haven	19	7	14	19
Eldred	20	19	19	27
Branch	21	23	26	8
Porter	22	16	24	17
Blythe	23	22	22	9
Pottsville	24	17	23	16
Pine Grove Bo.	25	20	25	23
Minersville	26	2	20	10
St. Clair	27	1	28	2
Fraily	28	29	27	15
East Norwegian	29	12	21	4

$Gamma_{1.2} = -.155$ $Gamma_{1.3} = .581$ $Gamma_{1.4} = -.011$

Table II-V

Shifting Political Balance Between Mining and Farm Areas, 1852–1868

	1852			1856	
	F	M		F	M
D*	11	3	D	9	5
W	3	10	P	6	8

	1860			1868	
	F	M		F	M
D	9	6	D	7	8
R	5	10	R	6	8

*The division made here is at the median rather than indicating which constituencies had actual Democratic or Whig majorities.

The main political thrust of the period rested in the Republican effort to unite all native Protestants within the Republican Party. Bannan constantly reminded his readers that the Republicans were the native party while the Democrats appealed largely to Catholics and "adopted citizens."[100] By the late 1860's, the Miners' Journal began listing the religions and family origins of their candidates in order to prove that no Irish Catholics were given candidacies by the Republican organization.[101] The Miners' Journal gave far more space to detailing the religious preferences of their local office seekers than to criticizing the actions of the Johnson administration, supposedly an issue of great importance to Republicans.

By 1870, Bannan was trying to convince the recalcitrant Germans that the Democrats were dominated by Irish Catholics and that they would be welcomed into the "Protestant Party."[102] He alluded to an Irish take-over which made it nonsensical for Protestants of any type to associate with the Democrats. He believed that if only a few hundred German farmers voted Republican the party could control the county. There can be no doubt that Bannan wanted the Republicans to isolate the Irish Catholics. He had been attempting to destroy this coalition since his days as a young Whig editor. The growing power of the Irish Catholics

---

[100] Miners' Journal, August 19, 1865, p. 3.

[101] Miners' Journal, August 31, 1867, p. 2.

[102] Ibid.

in the leadership circles of the Democratic party could be expected to
weaken German adherence to the party. Bannan and the Republicans stood
ready to capitalize upon any such rupture. One of Bannan's editorials
summed up the frustrations he must have experienced in trying to con-
struct a Protestant party:

> Protestants! Behold to what your supineness
> reaches. It is because the Evangelical
> churches are slumbering that Rome dares
> to come foreward thus. It is high time
> to wake out of sleep.[103]

During the three decades from 1840 to 1870 a number of changes
had taken place in the political alignments in Schuylkill County. In
the late 1840s the English minority moved out of the Democratic party
to be more than replaced by an inrushing horde of "wild Irish lads" in
the 1850s. Then in response to the Irish influx and the general process
of their assimilation into the Anglo-American culture, elements of the
German community left the Democracy to become a permanent part of the
Republican party. Traditional issues such as the tariff and slavery,
and traumatic events like the secession crisis and Reconstruction had
relatively little permanent effect on the political relations between the
county's sub-cultures which provided the building blocks of its political
coalitions. Certainly such issues did effect county politics in specific
short run situations during which they might spell victory or defeat in
one or several elections, but response to such issues did not form the
basis of political conflict in Schuylkill County during these years.

---

[103] *Miners' Journal*, Sept. 20, 1869, p. 2.

Chapter III

Party Leadership in Schuylkill County, 1844-1872

Americans may fondly believe that our egalitarian political system has permitted boys born in log cabins to become men who led our nation through much of its history, but the Abraham Lincolns were, in fact, far outnumbered by leaders born into affluence and security. In the past decade historians have shown that at most times during our national existence American politicians have been drawn from higher socio-economic strata than the rank and file voters who supported the parties in power. Social status greatly facilitated political advancement in the mid-nineteenth century just as it does today. As a consequence, the socio-economic differences between the leaders of the major parties in the nineteenth century are now generally viewed as having been quite modest.[1]

Despite this outward appearance of homogeneity, the leaders of the parties were often differentiated by more subtle factors, the most important of which was their religious preference. In Schuylkill

_____

[1] Paul Goodman, "Social Status and Party Leadership: The House of Representatives, 1797-1804," William and Mary Quarterly, XXV (July, 1968), pp. 465-74; James M. Banner, Jr., To the Hartford Convention (New York, 1970), pp. 365-66; Lee Benson, The Concept of Jacksonian Democracy (Princeton, 1961), pp. 64-85; Stephan Thernstrom, Poverty and Progress (Cambridge, 1964), p. 53; W. Wayne Smith, "Jacksonian Democracy on the Chesapeake: Class, Kinship, and Politics," Maryland Historical Magazine, XLIII (March, 1968), pp. 55-67; Edward Pessen, Jacksonian America (Homewood, 1969), pp. 251-54; Ronald P. Formisano, The Birth of Mass Political Parties (Princeton, 1971), pp. 42-47; and David J. Rothman, Politics and Power (Cambridge, 1966), pp. 111-36, 274-75. It should be emphasized that we are concerned with the social characteristics of party leaders, not the political affiliation of the county's socio-economic elite.

County, the "style" of religion practiced by Whigs or Republicans set them apart most clearly from the Democrats.[2] Thus, the real differences between the leaders of the two major parties in the county were not socio-economic but instead highlighted the effect of religious style on political behavior in the mid-nineteenth century. Religion also served as the major link between the leaders and the average voters of the county.

A. Whigs vs. Democrats

Major Leaders[3]

Three men unquestionably can be identified as the major leaders of the Whig and Democratic Parties in Schuylkill County between 1844 and 1852. They were Benjamin Bannan of the Whigs and Francis Wade Hughes and Robert Palmer of the Democrats. Bannan and Palmer commanded high positions because they edited the political journals of their respective parties during these years. Hughes was the acknowledged power of the county Democrats and had already achieved state-wide prominence.[4] These men were more widely known than the other county

---

[2] The term "style" of religion refers to the cleavage between "doctrinal orthodoxy" and "devotionalism" discussed in chapters 1 and 2.

[3] "Major Leaders" are defined as those who stood above the other activists of their party, and were men holding positions of great influence in the county organizations. For example, Benjamin Bannan, the leading Whig, edited the only Whig newspaper in the County. In short, the major leaders were in effect "party bosses". The "secondary leaders" were candidates, party officers or other party workers whose names appeared in the partisan presses of the era.

[4] Hughes served in influential state jobs and therefore had ties with leading state Democrats. It is further assumed that these state positions came partly because of his local organizing. Thus, his state power enhanced his local potency.

leaders and in positions to influence local party matters more than
any of their contemporaries.

Benjamin Bannan, the vituperative editor of the intensely
partisan Whig Miners' Journal, led the county Whig Party until its
demise in the mid-1850's, when he and his newspaper took up the
Republican banner. Bannan was born in Berks County in 1807 into a
Welsh farm family which had achieved a moderate level of comfort, but
was by no means wealthy.[5] The death of his father in 1815 forced young
Bannan to abandon farming and follow the printers trade. After serving
apprenticeships in the Philadelphia and Reading areas, he moved to
Pottsville in 1829 and purchased the then defunct Miners' Journal.
He retained at least part ownership of the journal for the next forty-
four years.

Although lacking a formal education, Bannan gained fame as
the leading authority on the economy of the anthracite region. During
his long and active life he wrote several books and a widely read and
highly respected column on the coal trade which he continued after he
sold the Miners' Journal until his retirement in the 1870s. A devoted
follower of Henry Clay, Bannan was most active in his support of a
protective tariff which he believed would boost and strengthen the
economy, provide more jobs and higher pay for labor, give to the farmer
a home market, and generally spur the spirit of enterprise. However,
as a fervent economic expansionist, he also gained some note in the
1850s as an advocate of a national paper currency. Bannan emphasized

---

[5] Munsell, History, p. 42. (The biographical material on
Bannan, Hughes and Palmer was largely derived from the same source.)

the complementary nature of the various elements of the economy, and
perceived the government's role as an active one in which public and
private enterprise would act together to create an environment of
economic opportunity.

The impact of the omnipresent Bannan cannot be taken lightly
primarily because he spoke for the county Whigs through the Miners'
Journal whose circulation exceeded that of the county Democratic paper
by a three to one ratio and once had more than 4,000 subscribers.
Financially, the Whig editor was quite secure by 1850. In the manuscript census of that year, he reported his personal estate at over
$8,000 plus ownership of his paper.

Bannan was a "self-made man" who had risen from a somewhat
uncertain childhood into complete fiscal solvency before the age of
forty-five. The zeal which typified the young publisher's financial
rise did not desert him in his later years and constantly proved to be
one of his strongest assets. Religiously, Bannan was a militant Welsh
Presbyterian who supported the "Benevolent Enterprise" of christianizing
ante-bellum society with the same fervor which he devoted to tariff
protection and easy money. Bannan perceived a direct relationship
between religion and politics and never could separate the two. Just
as his own economic success justified his faith in the nineteenth
century ideology of mobility,[6] his deeply felt religious views supported
his political crusades.

---

[6] Thernstrom, Poverty and Progress, 57-79, discusses views
very similar to Bannan's.

In many ways, Bannan reflected the qualities of the typical
Schuylkill County Whig of the era. He was from Pottsville, the strongest Whig voting district, battled on behalf of a high protective tariff,
idolized Henry Clay and was a devotionalist in religious style. Further-
more he became discernably anti-Catholic toward the close of the period,
and like most county Whigs, he gave increasing attention to temperance
and sabbatarianism.

In contrast to Bannan, his Democratic counterpart Robert
Palmer was born into considerable wealth. His father, Strange Palmer,
served as a judge and political leader in Schuylkill County. The Plamers
came from a well established background; in fact, they traced their
lineage to Miles Standish. During these years Palmer studied law, and
edited the Democratic Pottsville Emporium. As the Democratic editor
was the youngest of the three major leaders, he had been able to accumulate
only modest holdings by 1850.

Palmer was nominally a Congregationalist, but was secular in
orientation and cared little for the devotionalistic style of Bannan.
The youthful editor constantly avoided the political crusades which the
Miners' Journal supported. The Emporium rejected the nativist proposals
which its rival political journal gradually condoned and emphasized more
traditional economic appeals.

The county's most prominent Democrat was also extremely wealthy.
Francis Wade Hughes, an attorney by profession, was born in Upper Merion
Township near Philadelphia in 1817. The very prominent and financially
secure Hughes family actually settled in America before William Penn.

This ante-bellum "carpet-bagger" migrated to Schuylkill County seeking quick profits in the coal business and rapid political advancement in relatively unexploited Schuylkill County. He quickly achieved both ambitions.

Hughes' political and professional rise was meteoric. He studied law under the esteemed Pottsvillian, G.W. Farquhar, and became Pennsylvania's Deputy Attorney General in 1839 when he was only twenty-two years old. In 1843 Hughes was elected to the state senate from Schuylkill County.[7] Eight years later, Governor Bigler appointed him Secretary of the Commonwealth. Despite this remarkably active state political life, Hughes managed to direct the powerful Democratic machine of his native county.

Although he steadfastly devoted his life to "the party of the common man," Hughes was definitely not a commoner. By 1850, he reported an estate of over $36,000 and was regarded as an excellent trial lawyer and a highly successful economic speculator. Born to wealth, Hughes perceptibly improved his social and financial position after moving into the county.

Although of Welsh and French Huguenot descent, Hughes never identified closely with his religion.[8] Unlike Bannan he tended to compartmentalize his religious and political views. Hughes constantly pleaded for tolerance in politics and religion while opposing anti-

---

[7] During this senatorial campaign, Hughes received the largest majority ever given to an opposed candidate in the history of Schuylkill County.

[8] Munsell, History, p. 311. He may have been a Lutheran (Miners' Journal, October 23, 1885).

Catholic laws such as the naturalization restrictions then being proposed.[9] Basically a secularist, Hughes refused to support crusades for temperance and sabbatarianism and preferred to discuss long term Democratic programs like "reasonable tariffs" and currency regulations which would not favor "economic aristocrats,"[10] and struggled to divorce religious emotionalism from politics.

Some socio-economic differences then did set Hughes and Palmer apart from their Whig rival, Benjamin Bannan. The two Democrats came from prosperous family backgrounds and had more formal education. Bannan was older than both his Democratic rivals, but had not yet achieved the economic security of Hughes. However, all three men were clearly much better off financially than the average resident of Schuylkill County.

These minor differences between the three key leaders were overshadowed by the contrasting religious styles of the men. Palmer and Hughes, despite their affiliation with Protestant Churches, exhibited none of the crusading zeal which typified the devotionalist orientation. Bannan, conversely, was the very personification of "political Puritanism." The contrasting religious styles of Bannan and his Democratic counterparts became even more pronounced after 1850 when Bannan adopted a strongly anti-Catholic stance.

Secondary Leaders

Although close examination of Hughes, Palmer and Bannan offers

---

[9] _Emporium_, June 29, 1844, p. 2.

[10] _Ibid._, Sept. 30, 1843, p. 2.

insights into the differences between Democratic and Whig leaders,[11]
further analysis of lesser known political figures is necessary before
any final conclusions can be drawn. Thirty-one Whigs and twenty-seven
Democrats can be considered as their partys' secondary leaders in this
period.

Little appreciable difference existed between Whigs and
Democrats in regard to their ages, but the age distribution in the two
groups was quite different. The Whigs attracted slightly older activists;
however, 13% of them were also thirty years of age or younger in 1850
while only 4% of the Democrats fell into this category. Table III-A
shows that a majority in both parties were over forty, but a larger
segment of the Democrats (92%) were between thirty-one and fifty, while
only 62% of the Whigs fell into this age grouping. Overall, the Whigs
had a higher percentage of people in both the youngest and oldest age
categories while the Democrats dominated the middle age ranges. The ages
of the leaders did not clearly separate one party's leaders from those
of the opposing party. There were differences, but neither party in
the county could claim to hold a monopoly over younger activists or the
"old time" politicians.

The age differences, however, do assume some importance in
evaluating the relation between wealth and party affiliation. The
estates reported by the political leaders of Schuylkill County in the
1850 census allow us to compare the relative wealth of the two groups.

---

[11] In the remainder of this chapter, all men discussed are
"leaders." For example, the phrases "all Democrats" and "most Whigs"
refer to Democratic and Whig leaders not to rank and file voters. This
is done in interest of style since the word "leader" would otherwise
constantly appear.

Table III-A

Age Distribution of Democratic and Whig Leaders

Age Group	Democrats	Whigs
21-30	1 (4%)	4 (13%)
31-40	12 (44%)	10 (32%)
41-50	13 (48%)	9 (30%)
51+	1 (4%)	8 (26%)
Mean	39.9	42.8

Gamma= .141*

*Given the number of cases considered here and in the following tables a Gamma above .265 is statistically significant at the .01 level of probability.

Table III-B

Estate Evaluation of Democratic and Whig Leaders

Estate*	Democrats	Whigs
$0-999	8 (30%)	6 (18%)
1,000-4,499	9 (33%)	6 (18%)
4,500-9,999	3 (11%)	10 (32%)
10,000+	7 (26%)	9 (31%)
Mean	$5,011	$9,295

Gamma= .240

	21-30		31-40		Age Group 41-50		51+	
	D	W	D	W	D	W	D	W
$0-999	0	0	6	4	2	2	0	0
1,000-4,499	1	2	1	3	6	0	1	1
4,500-9,999	0	1	0	2	3	3	0	4
10,000	0	1	5	0	2	4	0	4

Partial Gamma= .176

*Wealth has been grouped in quartiles.

Although the majority of leaders of both parties were relatively
affluent, the Whigs had fewer poor leaders and a slightly higher
percentage of extremely wealthy chieftans.[12] For example, only 15%
of the Whigs had estates valued at less than $100; 19% of the Democrats
were in this category. On the other end of the scale, 6% of the Whigs
but only 4% of the Democrats held estates worth over $25,000. More
importantly, in the middle ranges the Whigs tended to be wealthier than
the Democrats, and the Whig average exceeded that of their opponents.
As Table III-B shows, there was a modest, but positive, correlation
between wealth and Whiggery. But the statistical difference between
the parties was a product of the small group of Whigs over fifty years
of age and the relationship between wealth and party nearly disappears
when one controls for the effects of age.

    The occupations pursued by the Whig and Democratic leaders
also revealed important differences between the party elites though the
vast majority of activists from both parties were anything but simple
laborers or yeoman farmers. The most notable differences between the
Whigs and the Democrats came among those men involved in the coal
industry. The Whig leadership circle included eight (26%) merchants
in all, but only four (15%) of the Democrats were merchants of any type.
However, five (16%) of these Whigs were coal merchants while not a
single Democrat shared that category. At the other end of the spectrum
two (7%) Democrats, no Whigs, were miners. Four of the Whigs (13%)
were attorneys while only one of the Democrats practiced law. Although

---

[12] This fits closely to what Holt found in Pittsburgh in
Forging of a Majority, pp. 47-48, 323.

both parties tried to recruit farmers into their leadership elites,
the Democrats maintained a slight six (20%) to four (13%) edge.
Neither party listed any clergymen among its leaders, but inn keepers
were prominent in both groups. As Table III-C shows there was only
slight correlation between a ranking of the occupational hierarchy
within the county and party affiliation, but the existence of a small
group of coal merchants among the Whigs stands out. Obviously historians
have correctly associated this group with the Whig party; yet they
constituted only 16% of the party's leaders, and with the exception
of this group, occupational differences between the majority of party
leaders were minimal.

Clearly, in the antebellum period, the leaders of both parties
in Schuylkill County could hardly be characterized as "average men."
Even in the party of Jefferson and Jackson laborers played a minor role.
Similarities between the elites of the two major parties are striking.
The "typical" Whig was slightly older, wealthier, and more commercially
oriented than the "typical" Democrat, but the socio-economic differences
between the two parties were modest at best. The traditional view
which portrays wealthy Whigs opposing poor Democrats cannot be sustained
by the evidence from Schuylkill County. Both parties were led by men
of ample means accompanied by a smattering of the county's patricians,
and the plebians of Schuylkill could do little else but weild their
suffrage rights on election days.

If the leaders of the two parties did not differ significantly
in terms of age, wealth and occupation, they did exhibit marked ethnic

Table III-C

Occupational Grouping of Democratic and Whig Leaders

Occupational Group	Democrats	Whigs
Unskilled laborers*	10 (37%)	8 (25%)
Skilled laborers	4 (15%)	6 (19%)
Low white collar	2 (7%)	4 (12%)
Business and Professional	11 (41%)	14 (43%)

Gamma= .141

*This category includes the farmers among the leaders although they were generally wealthy men. This is particularly true among the Democrats. The heirarchy constructed here follows that of Thernstrom.

Table III-D

Ethno-religious Grouping of Democratic and Whig Leaders

Ethnic Group	Democrats	Whigs	% Democratic within the group
Irish	2 (7%)	0 (0%)	100
Germans	15 (55%)	11 (35%)	58
English**	9 (35%)	13 (42%)	41
Welsh	1 (3%)	7 (23%)	12

Gamma= .550

Wealth

	$0-999		1,000-4,499		4,500-9,999		10,000+	
	D	W	D	W	D	W	D	W
Irish	2	0	0	0	0	0	0	0
Germans	4	4	6	1	1	3	4	3
English	2	1	4	5	1	5	2	2
Welsh	0	1	0	0	0	2	1	4

Partial Gamma= .562

**This group includes four Scots; three were Whigs and one a Democrat.

and religious contrasts.[13] The Whigs were essentially led by men of

Welsh and English family backgrounds who tended to belong to the more

devotionalistic Protestant sects. Over 70% of the Whig leaders came

from these two groups while not a single Irish Catholic could be found

in the Whig elite. Conversely, only 41% of the Democrats were Welsh

or English, but 7% of the Democrats were Irish Catholics. The Germans

obviously found the Democratic party more compatable than the Whig

organization. They made up 48% of the Democratic leadership and only

26% of the Whig hierarchy. To put the matter differently 90% of the

Welsh leaders and 58% of the English were Whigs, while 62% of the Germans

and 100% of the Irish were Democrats.

Although the evidence here is based upon ethnic derivation of

names, it has already been demonstrated that in Schuylkill County ethnicity

also indicated religious orientation. If the four major population groups

are ranked on an ordinal scale in terms of their tendency toward "devotion-

alism" or "doctrinal orthodoxy," the correlation between their position

on that scale and the groups political commitment is strong. This

relationship is stranger than any other seen thusfar and continues to

hold if one controls for wealth (Table III-D). The Democratic Party was

the more cosmopolitan party at this juncture. Its leaders were largely

of German and English ancestry, but two Irish Catholics, and a Welsh

---

[13] All but one of the 31 of the Whig leaders, for example,
were native born. Only 2 of the Democrats were foreign born. In this
chapter, the terms "Welsh leader", "German politician", "Irish activist",
etc., mean that the leaders were native citizens of these ethnic backgrounds not that they were foreign born. We are attempting to relate them
to the major sub-cultures within the county which clustered around ethnic
associations such as churches and fraternal orders and were knit together
by marital and familial ties.

Protestant were also included in its ruling elite. The Democrats,
were clearly more tolerant and, as a result, attracted leaders from
a wider ethno-religious spectrum. The Whig leaders were members of
a "devotionalistic club" which all but prohibited both the "doctrinally
orthodox" and the secularly oriented.

This ethno-religious factor was so powerful that it transcended the native-foreign born dichotomy completely. The leaders of both
parties were nearly universally native born, but the only foreign born
Whig was from England while the Democrats had leaders who were born in
Ireland and Germany. Based on this evidence, it appears that place of
birth had little to do with determining party loyalties, but that people
identified primarily with their ethno-religious group once they arrived
in the county.

The secondary leaders then reflected the same differences
which had distinguished Bannan from his counterparts, Hughes and Palmer.
The Whigs tended to be devotionalists while the Democrats were more
doctrinally orthodox. This was the major contrasting point that set
the leaders apart from each other and united them with the followers.
No other bond functioned to connect the elite with the rank and file
in such a precise manner.

B.   Republicans vs. Democrats

Between 1853 and 1872 both Schuylkill County and the nation
witnessed the emergence of a new anti-Democratic coalition which used
many names, but eventually came to be called the Republican Party. An
analysis of the leadership of the two major parties during these years

reveals that ethno-religious factors effected the composition of these
party elites even more dramatically than in the previous period. The
heavy influx of Irish immigrants into the coal fields of the county
precipitated an outbreak of anti-Catholicism in the 1850s which pushed
the vast majority of the County's English Protestants into the nascent
Republican coalition. At the same time the county's economy was becoming increasingly diversified. The evolving nature of party leadership merely reflected these demographic and economic changes.

Major Leaders

The guiding light of the Democrats throughout this period
continued to be Francis Wade Hughes. By 1860 his meteoric rise had
not yet reached its zenith although Hughes had become one of the most
controversial and well known Democratic figures in the state of
Pennsylvania. He served as Democratic State Chairman during the
heated war campaign of 1862,[14] and no other Democrat was able to chall-
ange his domination of the county organization.

Hughes' financial fortunes continued to prosper during this
period. He listed his estate in the 1870 manuscript census at approximately $200,000. He was then fifty-two years of age and still pur-
suing an active law practice in the county. The Democratic chieftan
also dabbled in real estate development, coal mines, iron manufacturing

---

[14] Shankman, "Hughes and the 1862 Campaign," p. 383.

and even a visionary project designed to reclaim marsh areas of Long
Island and Staten Island.[15]

Politically, Hughes defended the rights of whites to prevent
the immigration of Negroes into their territories, condemned abolitionists for seeking to end slavery in the South,[16] and vigorously
opposed the nativist programs which permeated the politics of the 1850's.
He fully supported the controversial policies of the Buchanan Administration. In 1860 he followed other Buchananites into the Breckenridge
ranks ostensibly because he opposed Douglas' views on the tariff.
Asserting his fidelity to the pure dictates of the Constitution, he
became a Peace Democrat during the war, and an inveterate foe of Radical
Reconstruction.

The growing Democratic alignment with Catholics was exemplified by the appearance in the party's ruling elite of Bernard Reilly.
He was born in Cavan, Ireland in 1814 and came to the county in 1841
when he began the contracting business which provided economic security
until his death. He dealt mainly with the local railroads, often working
for the Reading Company. Reilly resided in Pottsville, and listed his
estate at $15,500 in 1870. Following his election to the state legislature
in 1851, he was appointed associate judge of the Court of Common Pleas.
In 1861, Reilly was elected to the Pennsylvania State Senate while also
serving as county mustering officer during the early stages of the Civil War.

---

[15] Munsell, History, p. 311a.

[16] Shankman, "Hughes and the 1862 Campaign," p. 391.

As late as 1872, Reilly ran for a Congressional seat only to be
narrowly defeated.[17]

Another Catholic leader of the Democrats was John W. Ryon
of Pottsville. Ryon did not arrive in Schuylkill County until 1863,
but he had previously achieved political prominence in his native
Tioga County. He served the county as a district attorney, state
legislator and Congressman. Ryon was forty-five in 1870 and possessed
a sizable $31,000 estate.

One of the few Irish Protestant leaders of the Democratic
Party during this period was the infamous opponent of the Molly Maguires,
Franklin B. Gowen. Gowen was only 29 years old in 1865, but by then
he had compiled an estate valued at $50,000. He remained active in
Democratic politics and attended the State Constitutional Convention
of 1872 as a Democratic delegate. He owed much of his political strength
to his connection with the growing Reading Company, but this association.
especially when combined with Gowen's haughty demeanor, eventually
limited his popularity.[18]

Robert Palmer, Hughes' former ally and co-leader of the
Democrats in the earlier period, suffered a heart attack and died in
the early 1860s. It is thus difficult to number him among the political
elite during these years, yet he is extremely important since he defected

---

[17] Ibid., p. 311a.

[18] In 1862, Gowen ran ahead of the county ticket when he
was elected district attorney; by 1872, he ran last among the Democrats
on the county ticket when he sought his delegate position to the State
Constitutional Convention.

to the Republicans in 1854 and received a foreign post from Lincoln.
This shift has been attributed to his response to the extension of
slavery[19] and was undoubtedly made easier by his English - Protestant
background. Palmer's switch typified the English flight from the
Democrats.

Benjamin Bannan continued to be the prime spokesman for the
opponents of the Democrats throughout the period from 1855 to 1872.
The switch of party labels from Whig to Republican did not appreciably
alter Bannan's ideology. He continued to support high tariffs and
sabbatarianism while condemning alcohol and Roman Catholics with equal
fervor. He firmly defended the Lincoln Administration's policies during
the Civil War and became an extreme advocate of the Greenbacks and
Radical Reconstruction. His political life had not left him a pauper;
his estate was listed at $113,000 in 1870, the same year which saw him
mark his sixty-third birthday.[20]

Lin Batholomew, an English Protestant, ranked as one of the
most prestigious of Republicans during this period. This former Whig
had become a member of the Schuylkill County bar in 1857 at the age of
forty. In 1860, he was elected to the state legislature and when the
war commenced a year later, served as aide-de-camp to Brigadier General
Wynkoop.[21] After the war, Bartholomew remained politically active and

---

[19] Munsell, History, p. 298.

[20] Bannan's estate rose appreciably because of successful
coal investments and his liquidation of most of his ownership of the
Miners' Journal by 1870.

[21] Munsell, History, p. 296.

served as a Grant delegate to the 1868 Republican Convention. He also was a delegate to the Constitutional Convention of 1872. Bartholomew never achieved the affluence of his fellow Republican leaders and listed his estate at $5,000 in 1870.

Three former Pottsville Whigs, Edward O. Parry, F.B. Wallace and Christopher Loeser, were also key Republican leaders. These three shared common attributes other than their former political affiliations. For example, all were wealthy men of professional status; Parry and Loeser were attorneys while Wallace was a printer-editor and the successor to Bannan as the publisher of the Miners' Journal.[22] A younger man, Robert Ramsey who was thirty-three in 1870, also emerged as a Republican leader during the era. He became Wallace's partner and listed his 1870 estate at a formidable $64,000. Parry was Welsh, Loesser German, and Wallace and Ramsey were both Scots.

A comparison of the key leaders reveals some striking contrasts and similarities. First of all, the six Republicans averaged roughly fifty-five years of age, eight years older than the four Democrats. Economically, these men knew financial success: two Republicans, Parry and Bannan, and one Democrat, Hughes, were worth over $100,000. Only one man, Republican F.B. Wallace, listed his estate at less than $1,000. Occupationally, all of the leaders were lawyers or editors. All resided in Pottsville which demonstrated the extent to which this one time boom town had come to be the hub of Schuylkill County political activity.

---

[22] Parry, a county judge, served as a vestryman in the Welsh Episcopal Church of Pottsville.

The men were all, except the youthful Ramsey, leaders of parties during the Whig-Democratic period.[23] This naturally accounted for the somewhat higher age average amongst the primary leaders. All of the Republicans were former Whigs, with the exception of Palmer, and all of the Democrats had been members of the same party between 1844 and 1853. Thus, former Whigs found the Republican organization the natural vehicle through which they could achieve their political goals and only English Democrats seem to have defected to the new party.

All of the Republicans except one were Welsh or English Protestants of markedly devotionalistic inclination. The four key Democrats, conversely, consisted of a Welsh Protestant, two Irish Catholics, and an Irish Protestant. As in the earlier period, the Democrats were more open to the advancement of Irish Catholics who were becoming the dominant element in the party. Once again, the most salient feature contrasting the major leaders of both parties was the style of religion with which the men were identified.

Secondary Leaders

The Republicans, like the Whigs of the earlier period, were older than the Democrats and Table III-E shows a correlation between age and party. The Democrats garnered half of their leaders from the age groupings below forty, while the Republicans listed only 32% in those categories.[24] Thirty-six percent of the Republicans, all former

---

[23] Of eleven politicians that appear in both groups five Whigs became Republicans and one—a German—defected to the Democrats. The ex-Democrats split with two—both English—joining the new party.

[24] This is similar to the previous period in which 35% of the Whig leaders were less than forty, and 48% of the Democrats in the 1844-1853 period fell below the 40 age mark.

Whigs, were fifty or older. The Democrats, who attracted leadership
from the ranks of Irish Catholic newcomers to the county, listed only
29% of their leaders in the 51+ grouping. These age differences reflected the dominance of former Whigs in Republican circles and the
growing importance of young Irish Catholics among the Democrats.[25]
However both parties continued to draw almost half of their leaders
from the 31-50 age categories (Republicans, 52%; Democrats, 48%).

Overall, the age of both groups indicates a persistence
of power in the hands of old leaders. When compared with the Whigs
and Democrats of the 1840s the average age of the leadership of both
parties increased markedly and both now included a group over 60
years of age (7 Democrats, 11 Republicans). The age distributions
offer no support for the argument that the Republicans attracted any
more of the younger people than did the Democrats.[26] It would appear
that the Democrats were the beneficiaries of increased activity among
the young.

The Republican leaders also tended to be notably wealthier
and somewhat "less poor" than their Democratic counterparts. For
example, only 6% of the Republicans had estates valued at less than
$100 while 19% of the Democrats fell below this line. Conversely,
20% of the Republicans and only 12% of the Democrats had estates valued
at over $25,000. Table III-F shows once again a modest positive

---

[25] Seven of the Democratic leaders under forty were Irish
Catholics.

[26] Professor Formisano reaches the same conclusion concerning the Republicans and Democrats in Michigan, see Formisano,
Mass Political Parties, p. 321.

Table III-E

Age Distribution of Democratic and Republican Leaders

Age Group	Democrats	Republicans
20-30	8 (12%)	10 (12%)
31-40	11 (26%)	14 (20%)
41-50	9 (22%)	22 (32%)
51+	12 (29%)	25 (36%)
Mean	42.8	47.1

Gamma= .248

Table III-F

Estate Evaluations of Democratic and Republican Leaders

Estate*	Democrats	Republicans
$0-674	13 (31%)	15 (22%)
675-5,499	12 (29%)	16 (23%)
5,500-17,999	10 (24%)	17 (25%)
18,000+	7 (17%)	21 (30%)
Mean	$13,117	$26,866

Gamma= .247

	Age							
	20-30		31-40		41-50		51+	
	D	R	D	R	D	R	D	R
$0-674	3	4	4	4	1	3	5	4
675-5,499	4	0	4	4	3	6	1	6
5,500-17,999	2	2	2	0	2	6	4	9
18,000+	1	2	1	5	3	8	2	6

Partial Gamma= .139

*Wealth has been grouped in quartiles.

correlation between wealth and party affiliation but this too practically disappears when one controls for age. The Republicans were
older and did inherit many of the former Whig leaders, while the
presence of the young Irish Catholics lowered the average holdings
of the Democrats.[27] The politicians of this era seem to have been,
in general, wealthier than those of the previous years, but the
relationship between wealth and partisan affiliation had not changed
greatly.

Although the two groups of party leaders differed little
in wealth, they were polarized in terms of occupation. Obviously
Schuylkill County's economy was becoming increasingly diversified
and a plethora of new occupations were listed by its political leaders.
The most startling change was the doubling in the percentage of lawyers
in the party elites. This phenomenon appeared in both parties with
equal impact. The Democrats included seven attornies (17%) among their
leaders, the Whigs thirteen (20%). Yet, lawyers accounted for nearly
two-thirds of all the Democrats in the "Business and Professional"
group.

As Table III-G shows there was a strong correlation between
rank in the occupational hierarchy and party affiliation. Nearly 60%
of the Democrats were either "Skilled" or "Unskilled" laborers while
an ever larger preportion (72%) of the Republicans held either "Low White
Collar" or "Business and Professional" jobs. In part this is accounted

---

[27] Of the eight Democrats (19%) who had less than a $100
estate, seven were Irish Catholics.

Table III-G

Occupational Grouping of Democratic and Republican Leaders

Occupational Group	Democrats	Republicans*
Unskilled	17 (40%)	9 (14%)
Skilled	7 (17%)	3 (5%)
Low White Collar	6 (14%)	14 (21%)
Business and Professional	12 (29%)	40 (61%)

Gamma= .560

*There were three retired Republicans (two Germans and a Welshman) who are not included in the statistical computations because their former occupations are unknown.

Table III-H

Ethno-Religious Grouping of Democratic and Republican Leaders

Ethnic Group	Democrats	Republicans*	%Democratic within the group***
Irish	18 (43%)	1 (+0%)	97
Germans	17 (41%)	24 (36%)	52
English**	4 (9%)	26 (38%)	19
Welsh	3 (7%)	17 (25%)	22

Gamma= .763

	Wealth							
	$0-674		675-5,499		5,500-17,999		18,000+	
	D	R	D	R	D	R	D	R
Irish	9	1	6	0	1	0	2	0
Germans	2	3	4	3	7	11	4	7
English	1	6	1	10	2	3	0	7
Welsh	1	5	1	2	0	3	1	7

Partial Gamma= .764

*There was one French Republican who is ignored in the statistical computations.
**Among this group there were four Scots, all Republicans.
***Adjusted for differing sample sizes.

for by the greater preportion of farmers - many of whom were quite
wealthy - among the Democrats (12% vs. 4%), but very real differences
did exist. These were most pronounced in relation to the county's
major industry. Although two Democrats (5%), the "ruler of the Reading,"
Gowen, and J.M. Wetherill of the famous Philadelphia family, were both
deeply involved in the coal business; nine coal merchants, a mine
supervisor, and a mining engineer could be found among the Republicans
(17%). In contrast, the Democrats included eight (19%) miners and
only one miner was a Republican.

The Republican leadership had a dispreportionate number of
businessmen of all types and included the only professional men (three
physicians and a Protestant minister) other than lawyers in either
group.[28] In contrast to the Whigs, the Republicans drew a much smaller proportion of their leaders from the ranks of "Skilled" artisans -
only impart because this group was disappearing. Also the percentage
of innkeepers among the prohibition leaning Republicans fell to 3%
while that among the Democrats remained at 7%. Clearly the leadership
for the new Republican party was business oriented while that of the
Democrats mixed lawyers and wealthy farmers with a growing element of
unskilled laborers.

In ethno-religious terms vast differences could also be found
between the two leadership groups. The Irish Catholics had literally
taken over the Democratic party. At the same time only one Irishman -
and he was very likely a Protestant-could be found among the Republicans.

---

[28] The remainder of the Democrats in the "Business and
Professional" group included two merchants and a wealthy "landlord."

In response to the emergence of the Irish and extreme polarization along ethno-religious lines had taken place. The English literally fled the Democratic party. Although they made up a smaller preportion of the Republicans than they had of the Whigs, they became as a group distinctly more anti-Democratic. The Germans who had supplied a majority of the Democratic leaders in the earlier period now uneasily shared power with the emerging Irish and they supplied approximately equal number of leaders for the two parties.

The Irish Catholics included among the Democratic leaders also caused the Democrats to be more heavily foreign born than the Republicans. Both groups included a larger number of immigrants than had the previous elites. Only 67% of the Democrats as compared to 85% of the Republicans were natives. The foreign Republicans came from Wales, Scotland, England and Germany; eleven of the fourteen foreign born Democrats were from Ireland with the remainder from Germany. Hence, even the leaders from abroad reflected the ethno-religious political polarization of the county. The Welsh and English tended to become Republican activists just as foreign born Irish Catholics became Democratic leaders.

The growing Irish Catholic power in the Democratic Party manifested itself most perceptibly during the 1872 county Democratic convention. At this gathering names like Furey, Igo, Murphy, Kehoe, Eagan, McCarthy and McGuirk dominated the proceedings. A Minersville Welshman, T.T. Davis, tried in vain for nomination to a county office

and was beaten on the third ballot.[30] The Democrats still gave nominations to German Lutheran candidates; Peter Miller of East Brunswick
Township, for example, defeated Davis. Yet, Germans did not receive the
number of nominations they had once garnered at Democratic conventions.
The Irish were no longer just following. They now demanded a major
share of the leadership in the Democratic Party of Schuylkill County.

Tables III-H show the strong correlation between the ethno-
religious factor and party affiliation which remains even when one
controls for the effect of wealth. However, the effect of occupation
presents a more difficult problem. As a social structure emerged in
the county, the occupational hierarchy tended to follow ethnic lines.
To reverse the words of Rowland Berthoff; ethno-religious groups were
becoming the social classes of the anthracite region.[31] As Table III-I
shows there was a correlation between ethno-religious groups and the
occupational hierarchy among Schuylkill County political leaders.
Certainly this dimension of economic difference did distinguish the
elites of the two parties, but if one controls for occupation the
correlation between ethno-religious group and party affiliation remains
extremely high. To a far greater extent than in the previous group,
occupational differences distinguished the Republicans from the Democrats,

---

[30] Miners' Journal, August 28, 1872, p.2.

[31] Rowland Berthoff, "The Social Order of the Anthracite
Region, 1825–1902," Pennsylvania Magazine of History and Biography,
LXXXIX (July, 1965), p. 274.

Table III-I

Occupation and Ethno-religious Grouping Among Party Leaders

	Unskilled	Skilled	Low White Collar	Business and Professional
Irish	10 (38%)	2 (20%)	3 (16%)	4 (8%)
Germans	10 (38%)	6 (60%)	8 (42%)	17 (33%)
English	2 (8%)	2 (20%)	5 (26%)	19 (37%)
Welsh	4 (15%)	0	3 (16%)	12 (23%)

Gamma= .409

	Irish		Germans		English		Welsh	
	D	R	D	R	D	R	D	R
Unskilled	9	1	5	5	1	1	2	2
Skilled	2	0	4	2	1	1	0	0
Low White Collar	3	0	3	5	0	5	0	3
Business and Professional	4	0	5	12	2	17	1	11

Partial Gamma= .360

	Unskilled*		Skilled		Low White Collar		Business and Professional	
	D	R	D	R	D	R	D	R
Irish	9	1	2	0	3	0	4	0
Germans	5	5	4	2	3	5	5	12
English	1	1	1	1	0	5	2	17
Welsh	2	2	0	0	0	3	1	11

Partial Gamma= .716

*Among this category were seven famers; six Germans divided equally between the two parties, and one Welsh Democrat.

but the ethno-religious factor had become even more important than
it had been in the earlier period.

While the leaders of both parties continued to be men of
above average-wealth and social standing, greater differences existed
between the Republican and Democratic elites than those in the earlier
period. The rise of the Irish and the flight of the English from the
Democratic party marked the most striking contrast between the two
periods. The emergent Irish Catholics who now constituted nearly half
of the Democrats made that party's "typical" leader younger, poorer,
less likely to be a businessman, and more apt to be foreign born than
his Republican counterpart. The Democratic leadership represented a
troubled misalliance between two quite dissimilar groups: the urban
Irish Catholics and the rural German Lutherans.[32] The former included
a relatively poor laboring element while the latter were generally
quite well off. They did share a common religious style, "doctrinal
orthodoxy;" and in their attempts to maintain their familiar customs
and life styles, they faced a common foe, those groups trying to force
upon the county the mores of Anglo-Protestant culture. Although an
occupational polarization which had not previously existed divided the
Republican and Democratic leaders, it served mainly to reinforce the
ethno-religious contrast between the two groups which remained the
leaders most important link with the voters.

---

[32] Not only did the Germans make up all of the Democratic
farmers but they included a tanner who also farmed and a wealthy
"landlord" who were respectively included in the "skilled" and
"Business and Professional" categories.

Chapter IV

Conclusion

Although the assimilation of its various ethno-religious groups
has totally altered its political structure, Schuylkill County remains
today an area in which the ethno-religious factor weilds a modicum of
influence. Both contemporary parties are conscious of placing the proper
ethnic names somewhere on local tickets. A recent feud which split the
county's Democratic organization emerged primarily because of assertions of
"Irish dominance" of the established party elite. Hence, the controversey
of 1872 seemed to be repeating itself one hundred years later. But the
ethno-religious factor no longer dominates local politics as it did during
the years surveyed here.[1] National questions of the period served generally
to intensify ethno-religious antagonisms or at best produce momentary deviant
situations. Any attempt to explain mid-nineteenth century electoral politics
in the county either on the basis of national issues or in terms of traditional
conceptions of economic class would be totally inadequate.

Fragmented geographically, economically and culturally, the most
distinctive elements of Schuylkill County's nascent social structure were
its four major ethnic groups. National churches and fraternal orders provided the "institutional nucleus" for fairly stable ethnic communities which
maintained traditional cultural values and generally resisted social mixture
with each other.[2] Throughout this period the political preference of these

---

[1]Richard L. Kolbe, "Culture, Political Parties and Voting Behavior:
Schuylkill County," Polity, VIII (Winter, 1975), pp. 241-68.

[2]Berthoff, "The Social Order of the Anthracite Region," is the
basis for most of this discussion.

groups is easily identified and the political coalitions which emerged can best be explained in terms shared aspects of the life-styles of the sub-cultures related to their religious outlooks.

The least unified of these four groups were those we have called the English Protestants. Made up of native born and immigrant groups of English dissent, they ranged across the religious spectrum clustering toward devotionalism. Although a large number of them were involved in some aspect of the mining business, they could be found in nearly all occupational groups in the county. The county's English Protestants generally opposed the Democratic party in the early 1840s, and their opposition grew more pronounced after the Walker Tariff and increased during the period of rising anti-Catholicism in the 1850s. The appeal of the Republican party's programs and character to this group ended any appreciable affiliation with the Democrats.

The most firmly Whig and Republican group were the Welsh Protestants. As an ethnic group which was repeatedly renewed by continuing immigration, they remained tightly knit throughout this period. However to a greater degree than any of the other groups they were being assimilated by the English Protestants. Religiously the Welsh were extreme devotionalists. Although most Welsh had come to the county as miners and they continued to make up a large element of those working inside the mines, the process of social mobility had eleveated many of them to positions of higher status both in the mining industry and other businesses.[3]

-----

[3]On the English and the Welsh see: Berthoff, British Immigrants in Industrial America.

On the other side, the counterpart of the Welsh in their partisan devotion were the Irish Catholics who provided the Democrats with their most loyal followers. Generally unskilled they worked as laborers in and around the mines. Religiously they were the epitome of doctrinal orthodoxy. As Irish voters came to play a greater role in providing the county's Democratic majorities, Irish Catholics steadily gained power in the party leadership structure until they appeared ready to thoroughly dominate the organization in the 1870s.

The other major element of the Democrats was provided by the German Lutherans who had heavily supported the party of Jefferson and Jackson since the late 1790s.[4] During these years neither the Whigs nor the Republicans were able to make serious inroads into this group. Predominately native born and farmers, these German Lutherans tightly clung to their traditional culture and its "doctrinally orthodox" religious orientation.

A small group of non-Lutheran, German Wesleyans were the only exceptions to the staunch German loyalty to the Democrats. These Germans generally lived in commercially oriented boroughs rather than in farm townships. Hence, their economic outlooks were different than their Lutheran bretheren. They also lived in less homogeneously German areas than did the county's Lutheran farmers. Roger Peterson, in a recent dissertation on Pennsylvania politics during these years, noted the differing political habits of the rural Lutheran and urban Evangelical

---

[4]Andreas Darpulen, "The German Element in Early Pennsylvania Politics, 1789-1800: A Study in Americanization," Pennsylvania History, IX (July, 1942), pp. 176-90.

Germans in other areas of the state.[5] Although typified by Charles Brumm,
who was born in Pottsville of German parents and moved up from an apprentice-
ship in watchmaking to a career in law and business under the tutelage of
Welsh politicians Howell Fisher and E.O. Parry eventually marrying into the
Anglo-Protestant group, many of these Germans may have migrated into the
area during these years.[6]

The political behavior of these ethno-religious groups in
Schuylkill County was closely related to their shared cultural perspectives.
Welsh and English Protestants, the strongest Whigs and later Republicans,
and the German Wesleyan sects could be classified religiously as "devotionalists." In contrast, although their cultures differed in many other ways,
both the Irish Catholics and German Lutherans were "doctrinally orthodox"
in religious orientation. Through their adherence to "negative liberalism"
county Democrats became the spokesmen of the doctrinally orthodox, while
the Whigs and Republicans expressed the political interests of the devotionalists in their quest to reform the morals of the society. This
polarization had completely solidified by 1872.

----

[5] Peterson, "Reaction to a Heterogeneous Society," p. 121.
See also: Formisano, Mass Political Parties, p. 299; Joseph Schaefer,
"Who Elected Lincoln," 51-63; and George H. Daniels, "Immigrant Vote
in the 1860 Election: The Case of Iowa," Mid-America, XLIV (July,
1963), pp. 142-162.

[6] On Brumm see: Munsell, History, p. 173. A recent seminar
paper at Lehigh University has shown the importance of immigrant German
merchants in a coal township just north of Schuylkill County, Thomas
Kline, "The Workers of Hazleton, 1850 to 1880."

The issues which served to divide the county parties were rooted in these differences. The Whigs and Republicans supported temperance, sabbatarianism, nativism and anti-Catholicism, programs to which a devotionalist could give strong political allegiance. The county Democratic party was openly hostile to such measures emphasizing limited governmental interference with mores and life style. While the two local parties often agreed on broader issues such as monopolies, the tariff and anti-Southernism, they never reached similar accord in regard to religious and moral issues.

The Republicans represented the Puritan party in Schuylkill County, a coalition of devotionalists who saw in Catholicism a danger to the society equal to those posed by "the slaveholder, the monopolist, and the social aristocrat."[7] The party attracted votes by condemning all programs associated with Catholics including liberalized naturalization laws. The Republicans would gain permanent political hegemony in Schuylkill County only when they managed to successfully isolate the Irish Catholics politically. The Republican rhetoric of the 1850's and 1860's indicated that they well understood that politics in the county represented competition between differing ethno-cultural groups. Hence, the party was properly focused for a county where ethno-religious voting determinism had for so long prevailed.

The political leaders in the county also reflected the local ethno-religious tensions of the mid-nineteenth century in Schuylkill

---

[7] This list of Republican enemies is given in the sketch of Brumm in Munsell, History, p. 173.

County. The Democrats were less commercially oriented than either the Whigs or Republicans, but they were by no means plebians. Generally, all political leaders of the period were men of better than average social standing. It was ethno-religious orientation rather than wealth or even occupation that provided the linkage between the voters and the political elite. The Whigs and Republicans were led basically by Welsh and English politicians, while the Democrats included significant numbers of Irish Catholics and Germans among their political activists.

National issues were able to disrupt normal voting patterns in the late 1840s and again in the 1860s, but they had little effect upon the county's political structure in the long run. Further there was an urban/rural split between the parties in the 1840s and obviously some occupational differences between the Republicans and the Democrats in the later era. However, national issues and economic differences did not provide the primary basis of political conflict in nineteenth century Schuylkill County.

What was the relationship between these ethno-religious groups and social classes in the county? Defining social class in an empirically useful way is nortoriously difficult. A recent study of the county in a slightly later period distinguishes between three classes: the miners, the "new middle class," and the "classical bourgeoisie."[8] By the latter

---

[8] Harold W. Aurand, From the Molly Maguires to the United Mine Workers (Philadelphia, 1971), pp. 20-29.

two groups Harold Aurand means the local merchants and businessmen, and the mine operators. Central to class conflict during these years was, of course, the bitter battle between the miners and the operators over unionization. In this conflict, he argues that the middle class aligned itself with the workers against the operators who did not share their parochial interest in the county's economic well being and thwarted their social pretensions. However, it is not at all clear how this scheme which reflects real social conflicts in the county in the 1870s and 1880s can be fitted into the earlier period in order to explain partisan differences. Throughout our period both parties attacked the efforts toward the unification of the coalleries and Gowen and Wetherill who symbolize the later operators were both Democrats. A plausible argument is that the Republicans appealed to the "new middle class" of parochial boosters like Bannan who were generally English and Welsh, but also included a number of the urban Germans. Finally, few would doubt that at the bottom of the economic structure were the Irish Catholic mine laborers. Yet this presents real problems on several counts. It both fails to account for the German Lutheran farmers who continued to make up a majority the Democrats votes, and fails to supply nearly enough votes to explain Republican strength. Although they gained no Irish votes, the Republicans were strong in the coal regions because of the votes of Welsh and English miners. While it is true that the Welsh supplied most of the foremen inside the mines, the Welsh and the English also probably made up most of the "inside" miners in Schuylkill County during our period.[9] Thus,

---

[9]Berthoff, British Immigrants in Industrial America, pp. 46-61, discusses English and Welsh miners and on p. 50 gives the ethnic breakdown in a typical mine in the 1880s.

while there may have been a tendency for the Welsh and the English to
occupy the higher status mining jobs, "this hierachy was not rigid;" and
they were equally subject to the frightful conditions "Down in the Mines"
and the exploitation by the operators as were the Irish.[10] The majority
of Welsh and English miners did not live on the high side of the hill nor
were the only exploited poor clustered in Girardville or Wiggan's Patch.
It was not class groupings such as these — however well they might explain
certain forms of social conflict — which made up the coalitions which
battled in the arena of electoral politics during these years.

Although it has been important throughout the county's history,
the ethno-religious factor has been more important in structuring political
conflicts in some periods than in others. Paul Kleppner has proposed that
ethno-religious differences are most salient in culturally pluralistic
societies undergoing rapid social change and the patterns which he described
in the middle west at about this time are quite similar to those found in
Schuylkill County during these years. In the years before 1850 the county
was divided into separate geographical areas with different political
patterns. Ethno-religious differences were important to the degree that
such groups co-incided with these areas. However, as the pace of social
change increased and the population structure of the county was altered
by the influx of immigrants, particularly the Irish Catholics, ethno-religious
groups became an increasingly important source of personal identity for
people in the county and emerged as the primary determinant of political

_____

[10]Aurand, From the Molly Maguires, p. 37. On pp. 33-62 he gives a
brief discussion about the labor hierarchy in the mines and the opportunities
for economic mobility.

behavior. In the mid-nineteenth century Schuylkill County came to typify
the kind of social disorganization that developing capitalism and rampant
liberal individualism unleashed throughout the country.[11] In such a context
a heightened sense of "consciousness of kind" mixed with social and cultural
anxieties to produce a political situation in which the ethno-religious
factor achieved primacy. In the latter part of the nineteenth century,
economic and demographic change brought a major realignment in the county's
politics and in the context of this century the ethno-religious factor has
become less salient than it was a century ago.

---

[11]Berthoff used Schuylkill County as a micro-cosm of the social
disorder of nineteenth century America in his general history, An Unsettled
People (New York, 1970).

Appendix A: Presidential Vote in
Schuylkill County Minor Civil Divisions, 1832–1872

% Democratic

	1832	1840	1844*	1848	1852
Mahantongos	98	86	90	67	78
Union	100	84	83	82	85
West Penn	91	67	72	72	70
Rush	93	75	70	69	81
Wayne	91	66	69	62	69
Orwigsburg	84	67	67	56	71
Barry	71	80	66	49	77
Pine Grove Twp.	86	57	57	56	39
West Brunswick	–	–	66	48	67
Schuylkill Haven	74	62	66	45	53
Schuylkill Twp.	–	57	63	28	45
Tamaqua	–	60	59	40	43
Pine Grove Bo.	–	–	57	35	52
Branch	–	–	56	30	48
Blythe	–	–	53	38	48
East Brunswick	59	42	50	47	57
Porter	–	39	48	57	71
Manheims	–	–	44	47	62
Minersville	55	36	42	28	39
East Norwegian	59	35	41	31	37
Pottsville	39	29	39	28	36

*This uses stable geographic areas based on 1844 ranking. The returns here
are from the Miners' Journal.

	% Democratic					
	1852	1856	1860	1864	1868*	1872
Mt. Carbon	61	83	57	91	84	87
Mahantongos	78	86	70	81	78	80
Union	85	73	79	85	71	66
Norwegian	59	74	56	77	70	65
West Penn	70	74	63	74	68	63
Cass	66	77	56	82	67	60
Butler	65	59	24	55	67	62
Rush	81	77	43	76	66	41
East Brunswick	57	69	54	56	64	58
Wayne	69	65	48	63	62	59
Pine Grove Twp.	69	67	40	62	62	56
Schuylkill Twp.	45	52	42	48	60	55
West Brunswick	67	68	41	56	57	56
New Castle	42	62	46	64	55	35
Tremont	57	54	23	51	55	-
Tamaqua	43	53	39	55	52	40
Mahanoy	88	63	49	63	50	44
Orwigsburg	71	73	40	51	49	55
Manheims	63	34	41	38	48	46
Barry	77	54	39	52	46	47
Schuylkill Haven	53	50	37	45	45	39
Eldred	85	54	39	54	42	32
Branch	48	48	13	44	39	48
Porter	71	58	29	32	39	9
Blythe	48	67	28	51	37	29
Pottsville	36	44	28	38	37	30
Pine Grove Bo.	52	39	23	24	36	25
Minersville	39	44	33	40	36	42
St. Clair	42	52	33	39	32	38
Frailey	57	47	34	38	31	23
Norwegian	37	36	17	38	28	14

*This uses stable geographic areas based upon 1868 ranking.

Appendix B - Whig Leaders of Schuylkill County 1844-1853

Name	Home District	Age in 1850	Occupation	Estate in 1850	Probable Ethnic Affiliation	Birthplace
Benjamin Bannan	Pottsville	43	printer	$ 8,000	Welsh	Pennsylvania
Wm. Wolf	Pottsville	42	tanner	12,000	German	Pennsylvania
Andrew Mortimer	Pottsville	59	postmaster	2,000	English*	Pennsylvania
Issas Severn	Pottsville	40	carpenter	8,000	English	Pennsylvania
George Stitcher	Pottsville	45	merchant	15,000	Welsh	Pennsylvania
J.C. Neville	Pottsville	34	attorney	2,500	English	Pennsylvania
Thomas Williams	Pottsville	45	blacksmith	0	Welsh	Pennsylvania
Jacob Reed	Pottsville	25	coal merchant	20,000	English	England
Edward Parry	Pottsville	43	attorney	5,000	Welsh	New Hampshire
Sam Silliman	Pottsville	52	coal merchant	75,200	Welsh	Pennsylvania
James Silliman	Pottsville	58	coal merchant	20,000	Welsh	Pennsylvania
Benjamin Pomeroy	Pottsville	47	judge	10,000	English	Pennsylvania
Robert Ramsey	Pottsville	58	coal merchant	8,000	English*	Pennsylvania
George Wyncoop	Pottsville	28	contractor	8,000	English	Pennsylvania

*Probably Scottish or Scotch-Irish.

Appendix B (con't)

Name	Home District	Age in 1850	Occupation	Estate in 1850	Probable Ethnic Affiliation	Birthplace
Benjamin Pott	Pottsville	51	coal merchant	$30,000	Welsh	Pennsylvania
Jacob Kline	Pottsville	52	Justice of Peace	10,000	German	Pennsylvania
Joseph Graeff	Orwigsburg	32	inn-keeper	0	German	Pennsylvania
William Garret	Orwigsburg	36	clerk	500	English	Pennsylvania
Elijah Hammer	Orwigsburg	42	merchant	15,000	German	Pennsylvania
John Roseberry	Orwigsburg	30	attorney	1,150	English	Pennsylvania
William Koch	McKeansburg	40	farmer	700	German	Pennsylvania
George Dreibelbis	McKeansburg	45	inn-keeper	5,100	German	Pennsylvania
Henry Robinson	Sch. Haven	56	machinist	5,000	English	Pennsylvania
Fred Haas	Sch. Haven	55	inn-keeper	6,000	German	Pennsylvania
John Leyburn	Sch. Haven	35	merchant	3,500	English*	Pennsylvania
G.W. Pitman	Sch. Haven	34	mine foreman	5,000	English	Pennsylvania
John Reed	Pine Grove Twp.	33	farmer	2,000	English	Pennsylvania
Joseph Albright	West Brunswich	37	farmer	0	German	Pennsylvania

Appendix B (con't)

Name	Home District	Age in 1850	Occupation	Estate in 1850	Probable Ethnic Affiliation	Birthplace
Issac Betz	Mahantongo	41	inn-keeper	$ 0	German	Pennsylvania
Peter Filbert	Pine Grove Borough	56	coach line manager	8,000	German	Pennsylvania
Philip Osman	Mahantongo	30	farmer	2,500	German	Pennsylvania

Appendix C - Democratic Leaders of Schuylkill County 1844-1853

Name	Home District	Age in 1850	Occupation	Estate in 1850	Probable Ethnic Affiliation	Birthplace
Francis W. Hughes	Pottsville	33	attorney	$36,000	Welsh	Pennsylvania
Robert Palmer	Pottsville	30	printer	2,200	English	New Jersey
Charles Clemens	Pottsville	41	merchant	5,000	English	Pennsylvania
John Clayton	Pottsville	40	agent	12,000	English	Pennsylvania
Enos Chichester	Pottsville	56	physician	4,000	English	Connecticut
Thomas Foster	Pottsville	31	merchant	800	English	New Hampshire
Daniel Krebs	Pottsville	43	transporter	1,500	German	Pennsylvania
Joseph Woolison	Pottsville	45	tobacconist	1,500	English	Pennsylvania
Wm. Mortimer	Pottsville	40	merchant	16,000	English	Pennsylvania
David Klock	Pottsville	32	Justice of Peace	0	German	Pennsylvania
Joseph Weaver	Pottsville	42	stage owner	3,000	German	Pennsylvania
Bernard Reilly	Pottsville	31	coal laborer	0	Irish	Ireland
James Brailey	Pottsville	34	coal laborer	0	Irish	Pennsylvania

Appendix C (con't.)

Name	Home District	Age in 1850	Occupation	Estate in 1850	Probable Ethnic Affiliation	Birthplace
Michael Weaver	Minersville	43	inn-keeper	$ 7,000	German	Pennsylvania
Michael Beard	Minersville	44	wheelwright	1,200	German	Germany
W.J. Dobbins	Sch. Haven	32	druggist	0	English	Pennsylvania
Samuel Guss	Sch. Haven	48	farmer	4,000	German	Pennsylvania
Samuel Beard	Sch. Haven	37	mason	600	German	Pennsylvania
A.W. Leyburn	Sch. Haven	34	inn-keeper	3,000	English*	Pennsylvania
Stephen Ringer	Sch. Twp.	42	lumberman	10,000	German	Pennsylvania
Michael Fritz	Wayne Twp.	33	farmer	10,000	German	Pennsylvania
Samuel Boyer	West Brunswick	43	farmer	10,000	German	Pennsylvania
Christian Straub	Orwigsburg	48	sheriff	0	German	Pennsylvania
Lewis Dreher	East Brunswick	50	farmer	800	German	Pennsylvania
Paul Lengle	Wayne Twp.	46	farmer	4,500	German	Pennsylvania
Francis Dengler	Barry Twp.	36	landlord	10,000	German	Pennsylvania
George Reifsnyder	New Castle Twp.	44	merchant	3,000	German	Pennsylvania

Appendix D - Republican Leaders of Schuylkill County 1855-1872

Name	Home District	Age in 1865	Occupation	Estate in 1870*	Probable Ethnic Affiliation	Birthplace
Benjamin Bannan	Pottsville	58	printer	$113,000	Welsh	Pennsylvania
Lin Bartholomew	Pottsville	48	lawyer	5,000	English	Pennsylvania
Henry Gressang	Pottsville	54	cabinetmaker	12,000	German	Germany
James Sillyman	Pottsville	72	lawyer	15,500	Welsh	Pennsylvania
Frank Pott	Pottsville	45	merchant	84,000	Welsh	Pennsylvania
William Fox	Pottsville	45	coal merchant	11,000	English	Pennsylvania
J.P. Hobart	Pottsville	72	retired	3,500	English	Pennsylvania
John Bannan	Pottsville	68	lawyer	85,000	Welsh	Pennsylvania
Christopher Loeser	Pottsville	71	lawyer	71,000	German	Pennsylvania
E.O. Parry	Pottsville	38	lawyer	125,000	Welsh	Pennsylvania
Daniel Shoener	Pottsville	43	lawyer	4,200	German	Pennsylvania
Lewis Reeser	Pottsville	49	Justice of Peace	6,500	German	Pennsylvania
John Conrad	Pottsville	65	Justice of Peace	5,400	French	France
Fred Beck	Pottsville	53	merchant	6,800	German	Pennsylvania

*If the person died before 1870 the 1860 figure was used.

Appendix D (con't.)

Name	Home District	Age in 1865	Occupation	Estate in 1870	Probable Ethnic Affiliation	Birthplace
George Wiggan	Pottsville	65	coal merchant	$110,000	Welsh	Wales
William Winlack	Pottsville	38	inn-keeper	500	English	Pennsylvania
Robert Ramsey	Pottsville	28	printer	64,000	English**	Pennsylvania
F.B. Wallace	Pottsville	36	editor	800	English**	Pennsylvania
J.A. Huntzinger	Pottsville	20	banker	31,000	German	Pennsylvania
John Werner	Pottsville	48	police officer-teacher	43,000	German	Pennsylvania
Daniel Christian	Pottsville	66	mayor	200	English	Pennsylvania
J.A. Passmore	Pottsville	29	insurance agent	7,000	English	Pennsylvania
Charles Pitman	Pottsville	65	retired	11,000	English	Pennsylvania
John Roseberry	Pottsville	50	lawyer	43,000	English	Pennsylvania
C.W. Clemens	Pottsville	55	manufacturer	24,000	English	Pennsylvania
John Heebner	Pottsville	29	clerk	5,500	German	Pennsylvania
George Wiggan, Jr.	Tamaqua	44	coal merchant	33,000	Welsh	Pennsylvania

**Probably Scottish or Scotch-Irish

Appendix D (con't.)

Name	Home District	Age in 1865	Occupation	Estate in 1870	Probable Ethnic Affiliation	Birthplace
Jacob Stitcher	Tamaqua	49	merchant	$ 1,750	Welsh	Pennsylvania
Howell Fisher	Minersville	40	lawyer	600	Welsh	Pennsylvania
C.W. Taylor	Minersville	54	magistrate	3,600	English	Pennsylvania
Joseph Bowan	Minersville	57	landlord	600	Welsh	Pennsylvania
Lewis C. Dougherty	Minersville	58	coal merchant	300	Irish	Pennsylvania
Seth Geer	Minersville	35	lawyer	700	Welsh	Pennsylvania.
Samuel Kaufman	Minersville	35	teamster	100	German	Pennsylvania
Benjamin Griffith	Ashland	43	clerk	600	Welsh	Pennsylvania
A.P. Spinney	Ashland	37	lawyer	500	English	Pennsylvania
Evan Thomas	Washington Twp.	55	retired	5,600	Welsh	Pennsylvania
John Conrad	Washington Twp.	60	farmer	6,500	German	Pennsylvania
Dr. A. Schultz	Auburn	65	physician	1,000	German	Germany
Daniel Koch	Auburn	50	farmer	9,700	German	Pennsylvania

Appendix D (con't.)

Name	Home District	Age in 1865	Occupation	Estate in 1870	Probable Ethnic Affiliation	Birthplace
Henry Saylor	Sch. Haven	50	banker	$ 10,500	German	Pennsylvania
Dr. P.R. Palm	Sch. Haven	40	physician	2,200	English	Pennsylvania
William Schall	Orwigsburg	38	merchant	18,000	German	Pennsylvania
George McCabe	Orwigsburg	41	lawyer	22,000	English**	Pennsylvania
Samuel Madden	Orwigsburg	41	coal merchant	675	English	Pennsylvania
Jacob Hammer	Orwigsburg	62	store manager	5,500	German	Pennsylvania
Eli Thompson	Norwegian Twp.	50	agent	600	Welsh	Pennsylvania
Dr. R.H. Coryell	St. Clair	47	physician	162,000	English	Pennsylvania
H.C. Jackson	St. Clair	54	merchant	100	English	England
J.B. Reed	St. Clair	51	magistrate	900	English	Pennsylvania
John Devy	Blythe Twp.	46	mining engineer	500	English	England
Cyrus Pinkerton	Tremont Boro.	39	lawyer	2,600	English	Pennsylvania
Fred Haesler	W. Brunswick Twp.	51	farmer	6,000	German	Germany

Appendix D (con't.)

Name	Home District	Age in 1865	Occupation	Estate in 1870	Probable Ethnic Affiliation	Birthplace
Charles Focht	E. Brunswick Twp.	51	merchant	$ 4,000	German	Pennsylvania
Michael Kistler	Union Twp.	32	tanner	20,000	German	Pennsylvania
Abraham Heebner	Port Carbon	66	coal merchant	10,000	German	Pennsylvania
Jacob Wever	St. Clair	20	teacher	0	German	Germany
G.T. Jones	St. Clair	41	teacher	6,000	Welsh	Wales
Richard Brown	St. Clair	24	teacher	450	English	Pennsylvania
W.G. Burwell	St. Clair	47	coal merchant	3,000	English	Pennsylvania
John Parker	Mahanoy City	43	minister	2,000	English	England
John Davis	Cass Twp.	30	mirer	0	Welsh	Wales
C.N. Brumm	Minersville	27	lawyer	500	German	Pennsylvania
George Hehr	Minersville	45	confectioner	24,000	German	Pennsylvania
John Ralston	Tamaqua	34	mine superintendent	370,000	English**	Scotland

Appendix D (con't.)

Name	Home District	Age in 1865	Occupation	Estate in 1870	Probable Ethnic Affiliation	Birthplace
Henry Cake	Tamaqua	37	coal merchant	$200,000	English	Pennsylvania
Michael Beard	Tamaqua	53	inn-keeper	20,000	German	Pennsylvania
R.H. Stees	Pine Grove Borough	47	merchant	8,800	German	Pennsylvania
James Cleaver	Ashland	45	coal merchant	21,000	Welsh	Pennsylvania

Appendix E - Democratic Leaders of Schuylkill County 1855-1872

Name	Home District	Age in 1865	Occupation	Estate in 1870*	Probable Ethnic Affiliation	Birthplace
F.W. Hughes	Pottsville	47	lawyer	$200,000	Welsh	Pennsylvania
Jacob Kline	Pottsville	65	cabinetmaker	18,000	German	Pennsylvania
David Foley	Minersville	57	mine laborer	0	Irish	Ireland
Bernard Reilly	Pottsville	51	lawyer	15,500	Irish	Ireland
John Ryon	Pottsville	40	lawyer	31,000	Irish	Pennsylvania
F.B. Gowen	Pottsville	29	railroad president—mine owner	50,000	Irish	Pennsylvania
George Rahn	Ashland	72	judge	1,200	German	Pennsylvania
R. Wilson	Auburn	33	railroad fireman	450	English	Pennsylvania
Michael Cochran	Minersville	40	teamster	0	Irish	Ireland
James Ryon	Sch. Haven	33	lawyer	1,900	Irish	Pennsylvania
Ellis Hughes	Wayne Twp.	47	farmer	1,800	Welsh	Pennsylvania
Charles Hegins	Pottsville	52	judge	25,500	German	Pennsylvania
F.W. Conrad	Pottsville	30	lawyer	0	German	Pennsylvania
James B. Reilly	Pootsville	51	mail carrier	0	Irish	Ireland

*If the person died before 1870 the 1860 census was used.

Appendix E (con't.)

Name	Home District	Age in 1865	Occupation	Estate in 1870	Probable Ethnic Affiliation	Birthplace
Francis Bechtel	Pottsville	28	lawyer	$ 5,000	German	Pennsylvania
J.M. Wetherill	Pottsville	37	mine agent	12,200	English	Pennsylvania
Richard Rahn	Pottsville	31	clerk	500	German	Pennsylvania
Solomon Foster, Jr.	Pottsville	20	lawyer	3,000	English	Pennsylvania
William McCarthy	St. Clair	25	hotel keeper	850	Irish	Pennsylvania
Valentine Benner	Mahanoy City	30	hotel keeper	4,300	German	Germany
John Murphy	East Nor. Twp.	61	mine laborer	600	Irish	Ireland
Francis McGuirk	East Nor. Twp.	30	mine laborer	0	Irish	Ireland
Tom Eagan	Cass Twp.	21	mine laborer	0	Irish	Ireland
T.T. Davis	Minersville	66	mine laborer	400	Welsh	Wales
William Gensemer	Sch. Haven	45	merchant	11,000	German	Pennsylvania
Richard Curnow	Tamaqua	45	mine laborer	800	German	Pennsylvania
Charles Miller	Tamaqua	43	tailor	21,000	German	Germany
W.H. Uhler	Pine Grove Boro.	29	merchant	10,000	German	Pennsylvania

Appendix E (con't.)

Name	Home District	Age in 1865	Occupation	Estate in 1870	Probable Ethnic Affiliation	Birthplace
Charles King	Ashland	45	tavern keeper	$ 11,000	English	Pennsylvania
Mike Igo	Ashland	41	mine laborer	0	Irish	Ireland
Daniel Boyer	North Manheim	29	surveyor	12,000	German	Pennsylvania
J.B. McCamant	Shenandoah	35	bank cashier	3,000	Irish	Pennsylvania
Charles Dougherty	Cressona	36	carpenter	1,700	Irish	Pennsylvania
Richard Nash	Cressona	32	machinist	1,700	Irish	Ireland
John Dowling	Pottsville	50	boatman	4,500	Irish	Ireland
Peter Mudey	Pottsville	68	clerk	400	Irish	Pennsylvania
Daniel Weaver	East Brunswick Twp.	72	farmer	17,500	German	Pennsylvania
Joseph Maurer	Eldred Twp.	44	farmer	51,000	German	Pennsylvania
Valentine Savidge	Eldred Twp.	63	farmer	15,000	German	Pennsylvania
Michael Beard	Tamaqua	55	landlord	10,500	German	Pennsylvania
J. Frederici	West Penn Twp.	34	tanner & farmer	8,000	German	Pennsylvania
Jack Kehoe	Shenandoah	35	mine laborer	0	Irish	Ireland

Appendix F - Sources for Information on Party Leaders

The information contained in appendices B, C, D and E
was obtained primarily from Manuscript Population Census Schedules
of the United States for the years 1850, 1860 and 1870, supplimented
by biographical data from the volumes by Munsell, Boyd, Wiley and
Zerby. Basically, the political newspapers of the county were first
searched for the names of party activists: men who held county party
positions, ran as candidates, or were participants in county political
conventions or meetings. Once a list of these names was compiled,
county histories and the census were scanned in an attempt to locate
as many of these men as possible. Approximately 50% of the original
names were located. Although little can be said about the "unknowns,"
there was little difference between the proportion of Democrats in that
group when compared to those we were able to locate. The larger size
of the anti-Democratic groups, especially the Republicans,was a product
of the sources available. The only sustained newspaper run for this
period is that of the Miner's Journal.

Some difficulties were involved in this process. First, the
census information was on microfilm which was often unclear and difficult
to decipher. For example, no page numbers appeared in any consistent
form for Schuylkill County's population in any of the reports. Secondly,
a person was extremely difficult to locate if his exact district of
residence was unknown. Lastly, a section of census information at times
appeared for which no town or township name was given. These and other
minor problems combined with the notorious mobility of nineteenth century

Americans to prevent the location of all names found in the newspapers;
nevertheless, this method was certainly able to uncover a sufficient
number of political activists from which inferences could be drawn.

The census generally gave a person's age, occupation, estate
valuation and place of birth. Hence, the only information contained in
appendices B through E which was somewhat impressionistic is in the
"probable ethnic affiliation" column. A person's ethnic affiliation was
essentially assumed by studying his name. For example, the name Reilly
is generally of Irish origin while Davis is usually Welsh. Our basic
source for the national origin of names was the American Council of
Learned Societies, "Report of Committee on Linguistic and National Stocks
in the Population of the United States," Annual Report of the American
Historical Association for the Year 1931 (Washington, 1932), I, pp. 103-
441. Further information was derived by directly contracting present day
people with the same surnames of nineteenth century Schuylkill County
political leaders and inquiring about the ethno-religious origins of
their families. Finally, we were aided in our attempt to establish the
national origins of these names by David C. Amidon, who was raised in the
area and teaches Ethnic History at Lehigh University, and Jack Barton of
the Schuylkill Campus of Pennsylvania State University who is also a
Protestant clergyman in the county. While not totally accurate, these
methods certainly eliminated a high percentage of possible error.

Bibliography

Primary Sources

Manuscripts

Charles Graeff Papers, Historical Society of Schuylkill County, Pottsville, Pennsylvania.

Cristopher Loeser Papers, Historical Society of Schuylkill County, Pottsville, Pennsylvania.

Edward Kaercher Notebooks, Historical Society of Schuylkill County, Pottsville, Pennsylvania.

Edward O. Parry Papers, Historical Society of Schuylkill County, Pottsville, Pennsylvania.

Thomas Astley Papers, Historical Society of Schuylkill County, Pottsville, Pennsylvania.

Samuel Sillyman Papers, Historical Society of Schuylkill County, Pottsville, Pennsylvania.

Printed Sources

[Anonymous]. Reports of the Inspectors of Mines of the Anthracite Coal Regions of Pennsylvania for the Year 1872. Harrisburg, 1873.

_____. The Molly Maguires: Cut-Throats of Modern Times – History of the Blood Stained Crew. Tamaqua, 1876.

Boyd, W. Harry, Boyd's Directory of Pottsville with a Business Directory of the Principal Places in Schuylkill County. Pottsville, 1860-1880.

_____. Directory of Pottsville, Tamaqua, Mahanoy City, Ashland and Minersville with a Business Directory of Schuylkill County. Pottsville, 1867.

Chambers, George, Historical Sketch of Pottsville, Pottsville, 1876

Gowen, Franklin B. Statement of the Present Condition of the Philadelphia and Reading Railroad Company. Philadelphia, 1880.

Rupp, I. Daniel. History of Northampton, Lehigh, Monroe, Carbon and Schuylkill Counties. Harrisburg, 1845.

United States Bureau of Census, Seventh Census of the United States: 1850. Enumerated Census.

United States Bureau of Census, Eighth Census of the United States: 1860. Enumerated Census.

United States Bureau of Census, Ninth Census of the United States: 1870. Enumerated Census.

Newspapers

Pottsville Democratic Standard, 1861-1863.

Pottsville Emporium and Colliers' Democratic Register, 1843-1847.

Pottsville Miners' Journal, 1840-1880.

Pottsville Register and Democrat, 1850-1853.

Secondary Sources

Books

Allen, James S. Reconstruction: The Battle for Democracy, 1865-1876, New York, 1937.

[Anonymous]. History of the First Methodist Episcopal Church of Pottsville. Pottsville, 1930.

Auchampaugh, Philip G. James Buchanan and his Cabinet on the Eve of the Secession Crisis, Lancaster, 1926.

Aurand, Harold W. From the Molly Maguires to the United Mine Workers: The Social Ecology of an Industrial Union, 1869-1897, Philadelphia, 1972.

Barnes, Gilbert H. The Antislavery Impulse, 1830-1844, New York, 1933.

Beale, Howard K. The Critical Year: A Study of Andrew Johnson and Reconstruction, New York, 1930.

Beard, Charles A. and Mary R. Beard. The Rise of American Civilization, New York, 1927.

Benson, Lee. "Research Problems in American Political Historiography," in Mira Komarovsky, ed., Common Frontiers of the Social Sciences, Glencoe, 1957.

Benson, Lee. The Concept of Jacksonian Democracy: New York as a Test Case. Princeton, 1961.

Berthoff, Rowland. British Immigrants in Industrial America. New York, 1953.

Billinger, Robert D. Pennsylvania's Coal Industry, 1762-1954. Gettysburg, 1954.

Billington, Ray Allen. The Protestant Crusade, 1800-1860: A Study in the Origins of American Nativism. Chicago, 1964.

Bimba, Anthony J. The Molly Maguires. New York, 1932.

Binkley, Wilfred E. American Political Parties, Their Natural History. New York, 1943.

Blanchard, Paul. The Irish and Catholic Power: An American Inter-pretation. Boston, 1953.

Bonadio, Felice A. North of Reconstruction: Ohio Politics, 1865-1870. New York, 1970.

Bowers, Claude G. The Party Battles of the Jackson Period. Boston, 1922.

_____. The Tragic Era. Boston, 1929.

Bradley, Erwin S. The Triumph of Militant Republicanism. Philadelphia, 1964.

Brock, W. R. An American Crisis: Congress and Reconstruction, 1865-1867. New York, 1963.

Broehl, Wayne Jr. The Molly Maguires. Cambridge, 1964.

Burdick, Eugene and Brodbeck, Arthur J. (eds.). American Voting Behavior, Illinois, 1959.

Burnham, W. Dean. Presidential Ballots, 1836-1892. Baltimore, 1955.

Campbell, Angus, Philip E. Converse, W. E. Miller and D. E. Stokes. The American Voter. New York, 1960.

Carter, Hodding. The Angry Scar. New York, 1959.

Cave, Alfred A. Jacksonian Democracy and the Historians. Gainesville, 1964.

Cole, Arthur C. The Whig Party in the South. Washington, 1913.

Cole, Donald B. Jacksonian Democracy in New Hampshire, 1800–1851. Cambridge, 1970.

Coleman, Charles H. The Election of 1868: The Democratic Effort to Regain Control. New York, 1933.

Coleman, Walter J. The Molly Maguire Riots: Industrial Conflict in the Pennsylvania Coal Region. New York, 1936.

Conway, Alan. The Welsh in America. Minneapolis, 1961.

Coulter, E. Merton. The South During Reconstruction. Boston, 1937.

Cox, John and Lawanda. Politics, Principle and Prejudice. Glencoe, 1963.

Crandall, Andrew Wallace. The Early History of the Republican Party, 1854–1856. Boston, 1930.

Craven, Avery O. The Coming of the Civil War. New York, 1942.

_____. The Growth of Southern Nationalism, 1848–1861. Austin, 1953.

_____. The Repressible Conflict, 1830–1861. Baton Rouge, 1939.

Current, Richard Nelson. Old Thad Stevens: A Story of Ambition. Madison, 1942.

Curry, Richard O. (ed.). Radicalism, Racism, and Party Realignment: The Border States During Reconstruction. Baltimore, 1969.

Davis, Stanton L. Pennsylvania Politics, 1860–1863. Cleveland, 1935.

Dunning, William A. Reconstruction, Political and Economic, 1865–1877. New York, 1907.

Dusinberre, William. Civil War Issues in Philadelphia, 1856–1865. Philadelphia, 1965.

Eiselen, Malcolm Rogers. The Rise of Pennsylvania Protectionism. Philadelphia, 1932.

Eldersveld, Samuel. Political Parties: A Behavioral Analysis. Chicago, 1964.

Elliot, Ella Zerbey. Blue Book of Schuylkill County. Pottsville, 1916.

Fehrenbacher, Don E. Prelude to Greatness: Lincoln in the 1850's. New York, 1964.

Fite, Emerson D. The Presidential Campaign of 1860. New York, 1911.

Fleming, Walter L. The Sequel of Appomattox. New Haven, 1919.

Foner, Eric. Free Soil, Free Labor, Free Men. New York, 1970.

Formisano, Ronald P. The Birth of Mass Political Parties - Michigan, 1827-1861. Princeton, 1971.

Fox, Dixon Ryan. The Decline of the Aristocracy in the Politics of New York, 1801-1840. New York, 1919.

Franklin, John Hope. Reconstruction After the Civil War. Chicago, 1961.

Geary, Sister M. Theopane. A History of Third Parties in Pennsylvania, 1840-1860. Washington, D. C., 1938.

Gilbert, Russell W. A Picture of Pennsylvania Germans. Gettysburg, 1947.

Gillette, William. The Right to Vote: Politics and the Passage of the Fifteenth Amendment. Baltimore, 1965

Glazer, Nathan and Patrick Moynihan. Beyond the Melting Pot. Cambridge, 1963.

Glick, Elsie. John Mitchell, Miner. New York, 1929.

Grisham, Otto. The Greenbacks. Chicago, 1927.

Gusfield, Joseph R. Symbolic Crusade - Status Politics and the American Temperance Movement. Urbana, 1963.

Hacker, Louis M. The Triumph of American Capitalism. New York, 1940.

Hamilton, Holman. Prologue to Conflict: The Crisis and Compromise of 1850. New York, 1964.

Hammond, Bray. Banks and Politics in America from the Revolution to the Civil War. Princeton, 1957.

Hartz, Louis. Economic Policy and Democratic Thought: Pennsylvania, 1776-1860. Cambridge, 1948.

_____. The Liberal Tradition in America. New York, 1955.

Henning, D. C. and A. W. Schlack (eds.). History of Schuylkill County. Harrisburg, 1916.

Henry, Robert S. The Story of Reconstruction. Indianapolis, 1938.

Higginbotham, Sanford W. The Keystone in the Democratic Arch:
   Pennsylvania Politics, 1800-1816. Harrisburg, 1952.

Hofstadter, Richard. The American Political Tradition and the Men
   Who Made It. New York, 1964.

Holt, Michael Fitzgibbon. Forging a Majority. The Formation of the
   Republican Party in Pittsburgh, 1848-1860. New Haven, 1969.

Hyman, Herbert, Political Socialization. New York, 1959.

Jones, Eliot. The Anthracite Coal Combination in the United States.
   Cambridge, 1914.

Josephson, Matthew. The Politicos. New York, 1938.

Key, V. O. Politics, Parties, and Pressure Groups, 4th. ed. New York,
   1958.

_____. Public Opinion and American Democracy. New York, 1961.

Klein, Philip S. Pennsylvania Politics, 1817-1832: A Game Without
   Rules. Philadelphia, 1940.

_____. President James Buchanan: A Biography. University
   Park, 1962.

Kleppner, Paul. The Cross of Culture: A Social Analysis of Midwestern Politics, 1850-1900. New York, 1970.

Korson, George. Black Rock. Baltimore, 1960.

_____. Songs and Ballads of the Anthracite Miner. New York,
   1926.

Lenski, Gerhard. The Religious Factor. A Sociological Study of
   Religion's Impact on Politics, Economics, and Family Life,
   New York, 1961.

Lewis, Arthur H. Lament for the Molly Maguires. New York, 1961.

Lockard, Duane. New England State Politics. Princeton, 1959.

Lowi, Theodore. At the Pleasure of the Mayor. New York, 1964.

Luthin, Reinhard H. The First Lincoln Campaign. Cambridge, 1944.

McCormick, Richard P. The Second American Party System: Party
   Formation in the Jacksonian Era. Chapel Hill, 1966.

McKitrick, Eric L. Andrew Johnson and Reconstruction. Chicago, 1960.

McPherson, James. The Struggle for Equality: Abolitionists and the Negro in the Civil War and Reconstruction. Princeton, 1964.

Meyers, Marvin. The Jacksonian Persuasion. Stanford, 1957.

Miles, Edwin A. "The Jacksonian Era," in Arthur Link and Rembert W. Patrick (eds.). Writing Southern History. Baton Rouge, 1965.

Milton, George Fort. The Age of Hate: Andrew Johnson and the Radicals. New York, 1930.

_____. The Eve of Conflict: Stephen A. Douglas and the Needless War. New York, 1934.

Montgomery, David. Beyond Equality; Labor and the Radical Republicans, 1862-1872. New York, 1967.

Mueller, Henry R. The Whig Party in Pennsylvania. New York, 1922.

Mumford, John. Anthracite. New York, 1925.

Nichols, Roy Franklin. The Democratic Machine, 1850-1854. New York, 1923.

_____. The Disruption of American Democracy. New York, 1962.

_____. The Stakes of Power, 1845-1877. New York, 1961.

Nicolls, Wm. Jasper. The Story of American Coals. New York, 1897.

Parrington, Vernon L. Main Currents in American Thought. New York, 1926.

Pessen, Edward. Jacksonian America: Society, Personality, and Politics. Homewood, 1969.

Potter, David. Lincoln and His Party in the Secession Crisis. New Haven, 1962.

Pressly, Thomas J. Americans Interpret Their Civil War. New York, 1962.

Randall, James G. and David Donald. The Civil War and Reconstruction. Boston, 1961.

Randall, James G. Civil War and Reconstruction. New York 1937.

_____. Lincoln the Liberal Statesman. New York, 1947.

Rayback, Joseph G. Free Soil: The Election of 1848. Lexington, 1970.

Reed, John Julius. The Emergence of the Whig Party in the North:
Massachusetts, New York, Pennsylvania and Ohio. Philadelphia,
1953.

Remini, Robert V. The Election of Andrew Jackson. New York, 1963.

_____. Martin Van Buren and the Making of the Democratic
Party. New York, 1959.

Roberts, Peter, The Anthracite Coal Industry. New York, 1901.

Roseboom, Eugene. A History of Presidential Elections. New York, 1957.

Rosenberger, Homer T. Intimate Glimpses of the Pennsylvania Germans.
Waynesboro, 1965.

Roy, Andrew. A History of the Coal Miners of the United States.
Columbus, 1907.

Rupp, I. Daniel. A Collection of Upwards of Thirty Thousand Names
of German, Swiss, Dutch, French and other Immigrants in Pennsylvania
from 1727 to 1776. Philadelphia, 1898.

Schalck, Adolf and D. C. Henning. History of Schuylkill County
Pennsylvania. Harrisburg, 1907.

Schlegel, Marvin W. Ruler of the Reading: The Life of Franklin B.
Gowen, 1836-1889. Harrisburg, 1947.

Schlesinger, Arthur M., Jr. The Age of Jackson. Boston, 1945.

_____. The American as a Reformer. Cambridge, 1950.

Scrugham, Mary. The Peaceable Americans of 1861: A Study in Public
Opinion. New York, 1921.

Sellers, Charles G., Jr. James K. Polk, Jacksonian, 1795-1843.
Princeton, 1957.

Sharkey, Robert P. Money, Class, and Party: An Economic Study of
Civil War and Reconstruction. Baltimore, 1959.

Sharp, James Roger. The Jacksonians Versus the Banks: Politics in
the States After the Panic of 1837. New York, 1970.

Silbey, Joel H. The Transformation of American Politics, 1840-1860.
Englewood Cliffs, 1967.

Smith, Justin H. The Annexation of Texas. New York, 1941

Smith, Timothy L. Revivalism and Social Reform. New York, 1957.

Snyder, Charles McCool. The Jacksonian Heritage: Pennsylvania Politics, 1833-1848. Harrisburg, 1958.

Spies, William. The Pennsylvania Railroad. Philadelphia, 1875.

Stampp, Kenneth. And the War Came: The North and the Secession Crisis, 1860-1861. Baton Rouge, 1950.

_____. The Era of Reconstruction, 1865-1877. New York, 1965.

Steinhagen, Father H. J. Catholic Historical Book of Schuylkill County 1842-1917. Pottsville, 1917.

Suffern, Arthur E. Conciliation and Arbitration in the Coal Industry of America. New York, 1915.

Sullivan, William A. The Industrial Worker in Pennsylvania, 1800-1840. Harrisburg, 1955.

Swierenga, Robert (ed.). Quantification in American History: Theory and Research. New York, 1970.

Sydnor, Charles. The Development of Southern Sectionalism, 1819-1848. Baton Rouge, 1948.

Taussig, Frank William. The Tariff History of the United States. New York, 1893.

Thernstrom, Stephan. Poverty and Progress: Social Mobility in a Nineteenth Century City. Cambridge, 1964.

Thompson, Heber S. The First Defenders. Pottsville, 1910.

Troeltsch, Ernst. The Social Teachings of the Christian Churches. New York, 1960.

Turner, Edward R. The Negro in Pennsylvania: Slavery-- Servitude - Freedom, 1639-1861. Washington, D. C., 1911.

Turner, Frederick Jackson. The Significance of Sections in American History. New York, 1932.

Unger, Irwin. The Greenback Era: A Social and Political History of American Finance, 1865-1879. Princeton, 1964.

Van Deusen, Glyndon. The Jacksonian Era: 1828-1848. New York, 1959.

_____. Life of Henry Clay. Boston, 1939.

Wallace, Francis B. Memorial of the Patriotism of Schuylkill County in the American Slaveholder's Rebellion. Pottsville, 1965.

Ward, John William. Andrew Jackson: Symbol for an Age. New York, 1955.

Weaver, Gustine C. Welch and Allied Families. Cincinnati, 1932.

Weisenburger, Francis P. The Life of John McClean. Columbus, 1937.

Weller, H. A. Frieders Church at the Little Schuylkill. Pottsville, 1898.

Wiley, Samuel T. Biographical and Portrait Cyclopedia of Schuylkill County. Philadelphia, 1893.

Wiltse, Charles. The New Nation, 1800-1845. New York, 1961.

Wittke, Carl. The Irish in America. Baton Rouge, 1956.

Wood, Forrest G. Black Scare: The Racist Response to the Emancipation Proclamation. Berkeley, 1970.

Wood, Ralph. The Pennsylvania Germans. Princeton, 1942.

Woodward, C. Vann. Reunion and Reaction: The Compromise of 1877 and the End of Reconstruction. Boston, 1951.

Yearley, Clifton K. Britons in American Labor: A History of the Influence of United Kingdom Immigrants on American Labor. Baltimore, 1957.

_____. Enterprise and Anthracite: Economics and Democracy in Schuylkill County, 1820-1875. Baltimore, 1961.

Zerbey, Joseph H. History of Pottsville and Schuylkill County. Pottsville, 1938.

Articles

Albright, Raymond. "The Sect People in Colonial Pennsylvania," Pennsylvania History, IX (January, 1942), pp. 48-53.

Alexander, Thomas, et. al. "The Basis of Alabama's Ante-Bellum Two Party System," The Alabama Review, XIX (October, 1966), pp. 243-276.

Allison, Robert. "Early History of Mining and Mining Machinery in Schuylkill County," Publications of the Historical Society of Schuylkill County, IV (June, 1912), pp. 134-155.

Andrews, J. Cutler. "The Gilded Age in Pennsylvania," Pennsylvania History, XXXIV (January, 1967), pp. 1-24.

Anspach, Marshall R. "The'Molly Maguires in the Anthracite Coal Regions of Pennsylvania, 1850-1890; Being an Inquiry into Their Origin, Growth and Character and a Study of Absentee Ownership of the Coal Fields," Now and Then, XI (October, 1954), pp. 25-34.

Beale, Howard K. "On Rewriting Reconstruction History," American Historical Review, XLV (July, 1940), pp. 807-27.

_____. "The Tariff and Reconstruction," American Historical Review, XXXV (October, 1930), pp. 276-294.

Benson, Lee. "An Approach to the Scientific Study of Past Public Opinion," Public Opinion Quarterly, XXXI (Winter, 1967-68), pp. 522-567.

Berthoff, Rowland. "The Social Order of the Anthracite Region, 1825-1902," Pennsylvania Magazine of History and Biography, LXXXIX (July, 1965), pp. 261-291.

Brown, Ira. "Pennsylvania and the Rights of the Negro, 1865-1887," Pennsylvania History, XXVIII (January, 1961), pp. 45-57.

_____. "William D. Kelley and Radical Recontruction," Pennsylvania Magazine of History and Biography, LXXXV (July, 1961), pp. 316-329.

Burnham, Walter Dean. "The Changing Shape of the American Political Universe," American Political Science Review, LIX (March, 1965), pp. 7-28.

Campbell, Angus. "Surge and Decline: A Study of Electoral Change," Public Opinion Quarterly, XXIV (Fall, 1960), pp. 397-418.

Channell, G. W. "Port Carbon and Her People," Publications of the Historical Society of Schuylkill County, IV (June, 1912), pp. 156-167.

Coben, Stanley. "Northeastern Business and Radical Reconstruction: A Re-examination," Mississippi Valley Historical Review, XLVI (June, 1959), pp. 67-90.

Converse, Philip E., Angus Campbell, Warren E. Miller, Donald E. Stokes. "Stability and Change in 1960: A Reinstating Election," American Political Science Review, LV (June, 1961), pp. 269-280.

Cox, John and Lawanda Cox. "Negro Suffrage and Republican Politics. The Problem of Motivation in Reconstruction Historiography," Journal of Southern History, XXXIII (August, 1967), pp. 303-330.

Craven, Avery O. "Coming of War Between the States: An Interpretation," Journal of Southern History, II (August, 1936), pp. 303-322.

Daniels, George H. "Immigrant Vote in the 1860 Election: The Case of Iowa," Mid America, XLIV (July, 1963), pp. 142-162.

Dorfman, Joseph. "The Jackson Wage-Earner Thesis," American Historical Review, LIV (January, 1949), pp. 296-306.

Dorpalen, Andreas. "The German Element and the Issues of the Civil War," Mississippi Valley Historical Review, XXIX (June, 1942), pp. 55-76.

Downey, Edgar. "The Law Courts and Judges of Schuylkill County," Publications of the Historical Society of Schuylkill County, VI (January, 1947), pp. 1-41.

Dunbar, Willis F. with William G. Shade. "The Black Man Gains the Vote: The Centennial of 'Impartial Suffrage' In Michigan," Michigan History, LVI (Spring, 1972), pp. 42-57.

Dykstra, Robert R. and Harlan Hahn. "Northern Voters and Negro Suffrage: The Case of Iowa, 1868," Public Opinion Quarterly, XXXII (Summer, 1968), pp. 202-215.

Eastman, Elizabeth. "Early Days in Pottsville," Publications of the Historical Society of Schuylkill County, IV (June, 1912), pp. 185-192.

Elssler, Ermina. "History of the Henry Clay Monument," Publications of the Historical Society of Schuylkill County, II (June, 1909), pp. 405-417.

_____. "The First Presbyterian Church of Pottsville, Pennsylvania," Publications of the Historical Society of Schuylkill County, IV (June, 1914), pp. 394-406.

Ershkowitz, Herbert and William G. Shade. "Consensus or Conflict? Political Behavior in the State Legislatures During the Jacksonian Era," Journal of American History, LVIII (December, 1971), pp. 591-621.

Farquhar, Walter (ed.). "Schuylkill County in the Civil War," Publications of the Historical Society of Schuylkill County, VII (June, 1961), pp. 1-124.

Fishel, Leslie H., Jr. "Northern Prejudice and Negro Suffrage, 1865-1870," The Journal of Negro History, XXXIX (January, 1954), pp. 8-26.

Formisano, Ronald P. "Analyzing American Voting, 1830–1860: Methods," Historical Methods Newsletter, II (March, 1969), pp. 1–11.

Gatell, Frank Otto. "Money and Party in Jacksonian America: A Quantitative Look at New York City's Men of Quality," Political Science Quarterly, LXXXII (June, 1967), pp. 235–252.

Haas, James F. "An Informal History of Shenandoah, Pennsylvania," Publications of the Historical Society of Schuylkill County, VIII (January, 1965), pp. 6–27.

Hanney, Joseph M. "Pottsville's Early Days," Publications of the Historical Society of Schuylkill County, VIII (January, 1968), pp. 29–37.

Herbein, H. J. "Schuylkill Chronicles for the Year 1829," Publications of the Historical Society of Schuylkill County, IV (May, 1912), pp. 18–70.

_____. "Schuylkill Chronicles for the Year 1831," Publications of the Historical Society of Schuylkill County, IV (March, 1914), pp. 250–300.

Hobbs, Herwood. "The Origin of the Names of Towns and Townships in Schuylkill County," Publications of the Historical Society of Schuylkill County, VI (January, 1947), pp. 43–65.

Itter, William A. "Early Labor Troubles in the Schuylkill Anthracite District," Pennsylvania History, I (January, 1934), pp. 28–37.

Jensen, Richard. "The Religious and Occupational Roots of Party Identification: Illinois and Indiana in the 1870's," Civil War History, XVI (December, 1970), pp. 325–343.

Klein, H. M. J. "The Church People in Colonial Pennsylvania," Pennsylvania History, IX (January, 1942), pp. 37–47.

Kleppner, Paul J. "Lincoln and the Immigrant Vote: A Case of Religious Polarization," Mid America, XLVIII (July, 1966), pp. 176–195.

Leighton, George R. "Shenandoah, Pennsylvania; The Story of an Anthracite Town," Harpers, CLXXIV (1967), pp. 131–147.

Luthin, Reinhard H. "Pennsylvania and Lincoln's Rise to the Presidency," Pennsylvania History, LXVII (January, 1943), pp. 61–82.

Man, Albon P., Jr. "Labor Competition and the New York Draft Riots," Journal of Negro History, XXXVI (October, 1951), pp. 375–405.

Martin, Asa E. "The Temperance Movement in Pennsylvania Prior to the
     Civil War," Pennsylvania Magazine of History and Biography, XLIX
     (October, 1925), pp. 222-226.

McCormick, Richard P. "New Perspectives on Jacksonian Politics,"
     American Historical Review, LXV (January, 1960), pp. 288-301.

Montgomery, David. "Radical Republicanism in Pennsylvania, 1866-
     1873," Pennsylvania Magazine of History and Biography, LXXXV
     (October, 1961), pp. 439-457.

Nichols, Roy Franklin. "Some Problems of the First Republican
     Presidential Campaign," American Historical Review, XXVIII
     (April, 1923), pp. 492-496.

Paxson, Issac. "Reminiscences of Schuylkill Haven," Publications
     of the Historical Society of Schuylkill County, IV (May, 1912),
     pp. 71-92.

Pole, J. R. "Election Statistics in Pennsylvania, 1790-1840," Pennsylvania
     Magazine of History and Biography, LXXXII (April, 1958), pp. 217-219.

Powell, H. Benjamin. "Pennsylvania's Transportation Policy, 1825-
     1828," Pennsylvania History, XXXVIII (April, 1971), pp. 134-151.

Randall, James G. "The Blundering Generation," Mississippi Valley
     Historical Review, XXVII (June, 1940), pp. 3-28.

_____. "The Civil War Restudied," The Journal of Southern
     History, VI (November, 1940), pp. 439-457.

Raup, H. F. "The Pennsylvania Dutch of Northampton County: Settlement
     Forms and Culture Pattern," The Bulletin of the Geographical
     Society of Philadelphia, XXXVI (Winter, 1938-39), pp. 1-15.

Rayback, Joseph G. "The American Workingman and the Antislavery
     Crusade," Journal of Economic History, LIII (May, 1943),
     pp. 152-163.

Russell, William H. "A. K. McClure and the People's Party in the
     Campaign of 1860," Pennsylvania History, XXVIII (October, 1961),
     pp. 335-345.

Sanderlin, Walter. "The Expanding Horizons of the Schuylkill Navi-
     gation Company, 1815-1870," Pennsylvania History, XXXVI (April,
     1969), pp. 174-191.

Schlesinger, Arthur M., Jr. "The Causes of the Civil War: A Note on
     Historical Sentimentalism," Partisan Review, XVI, (October, 1949),
     pp. 969-981.

Sellers, Charles G. "Andrew Jackson versus the Historians," Mississippi Valley Historical Review, XLIV (March, 1958), pp. 615-634.

Shade, William G. "Pennsylvania Politics in the Jacksonian Period: A Case Study, Northampton County, 1824-1844," Pennsylvania History, XXXIX (July, 1972), pp. 313-333.

Shimmell, L. S. "The Pennsylvania Germans and the Common School Law of 1834," The Pennsylvania German, VIII (December, 1907), pp. 571-577.

Silbey, Joel. "The Civil War Syntehsis in American Political History," Civil War History, X (June, 1964), pp. 130-140.

Simkins, Francis B. "New Viewpoints of Southern Reconstruction," Journal of Southern History, V (February, 1939), pp. 49-61.

Smith, Edwin. "The Schuylkill Navigation Company," Publications of the Historical Society of Schuylkill County, IV (June, 1909), pp. 475-500.

Sullivan, William A. "Did Labor Support Andrew Jackson?," Political Science Quarterly, LXII (December, 1947), pp. 569-580.

Weisberger, Bernard. "The Dark and Bloody Ground of Reconstruction Historiography," Journal of Southern History, XXV (November, 1959), pp. 427-447.

Williams, T. Harry. "An Analysis of Some Reconstruction Attitudes," Journal of Southern History, XII (November, 1946), pp. 469-486.

Wolfinger, Raymond E. "The Development and Persistence of Ethnic Voting." American Political Science Review, LXIX (December, 1965), pp. 896-908.

Wood, Ralph. "The Pennsylvania Germans: Who They Are and What They Have Done," The Pennsylvania German, VII (July, 1906), pp. 145-207.

Dissertations

Aurand, Harold W. "The Anthracite Mine Workers, 1869-1897: A Functional Approach to Labor History," Ph.D. dissertation, Pennsylvania State University, 1969.

Coleman, John F. "The Disruption of the Pennsylvania Democracy, 1848-1860," Ph.D. dissertation, Pennsylvania State University, 1970.

Greene, Victor R. "The Molly Maguire Conspiracy in the Pennsylvania
     Anthracite Region, 1862-1879," M.A. Thesis, University of
     Rochester, 1960.

Petersen, Roger. "The Reaction to a Heterogeneous Society: A
     Behavioral and Quantitative Analysis of Northern Voting
     Behavior, 1845-1870, Pennsylvania a Test Case," Ph.D.
     dissertation, University of Pittsburgh, 1971.

Young, Henry B. "The Anthracite Coal Industry," M.A. thesis,
     Pennsylvania State College, 1924.

THE IRISH-AMERICANS

An Arno Press Collection

Athearn, Robert G. **THOMAS FRANCIS MEAGHER:**
An Irish Revolutionary in America. 1949

Biever, Bruce Francis. **RELIGION, CULTURE AND VALUES:**
A Cross-Cultural Analysis of Motivational Factors in Native
Irish and American Irish Catholicism. 1976

Bolger, Stephen Garrett. **THE IRISH CHARACTER IN
AMERICAN FICTION, 1830-1860.** 1976

Browne, Henry J. **THE CATHOLIC CHURCH AND THE
KNIGHTS OF LABOR.** 1949

Buckley, John Patrick. **THE NEW YORK IRISH:** Their View
of American Foreign Policy, 1914-1921. 1976

Cochran, Alice Lida. **THE SAGA OF AN IRISH IMMIGRANT
FAMILY:** The Descendants of John Mullanphy. 1976

Corbett, James J. **THE ROAR OF THE CROWD.** 1925

Cronin, Harry C. **EUGENE O'NEILL:** Irish and American;
A Study in Cultural Context. 1976

Cuddy, Joseph Edward. **IRISH-AMERICAN AND NATIONAL
ISOLATIONISM, 1914-1920.** 1976

Curley, James Michael. **I'D DO IT AGAIN:** A Record of All My
Uproarious Years. 1957

Deasy, Mary. **THE HOUR OF SPRING.** 1948

Dinneen, Joseph. **WARD EIGHT.** 1936

Doyle, David Noel. **IRISH-AMERICANS, NATIVE RIGHTS
AND NATIONAL EMPIRES:** The Structure, Divisions and
Attitudes of the Catholic Minority in the Decade of Expansion,
1890-1901. 1976

Dunphy, Jack. **JOHN FURY.** 1946

Fanning, Charles, ed. **MR. DOOLEY AND THE CHICAGO
IRISH:** An Anthology. 1976

Farrell, James T. **FATHER AND SON.** 1940

Fleming, Thomas J. **ALL GOOD MEN.** 1961

Funchion, Michael F. **CHICAGO'S IRISH NATIONALISTS,
1881-1890.** 1976

Gudelunas, William A., Jr. and William G. Shade. **BEFORE
THE MOLLY MAGUIRES:** The Emergence of the
Ethno-Religious Factor in the Politics of the Lower Anthracite
Region, 1844-1872. 1976

Henderson, Thomas McLean. **TAMMANY HALL AND THE
NEW IMMIGRANTS:** The Progressive Years. 1976

Hueston, Robert Francis. **THE CATHOLIC PRESS AND
NATIVISM, 1840-1860.** 1976

Joyce, William Leonard. **EDITORS AND ETHNICITY:** A History of the Irish-American Press, 1848-1883. 1976

Larkin, Emmet. **THE HISTORICAL DIMENSIONS OF IRISH CATHOLICISM.** 1976

Lockhart, Audrey. **SOME ASPECTS OF EMIGRATION FROM IRELAND TO THE NORTH AMERICAN COLONIES BETWEEN 1660-1775.** 1976

Maguire, Edward J., ed. **REVEREND JOHN O'HANLON'S** *THE IRISH EMIGRANT'S GUIDE FOR THE UNITED STATES:* A Critical Edition with Introduction and Commentary. 1976

McCaffrey, Lawrence J., ed. **IRISH NATIONALISM AND THE AMERICAN CONTRIBUTION.** 1976

McDonald, Grace. **HISTORY OF THE IRISH IN WISCONSIN IN THE NINETEENTH CENTURY.** 1954

McManamin, Francis G. **THE AMERICAN YEARS OF JOHN BOYLE O'REILLY, 1870-1890.** 1976

McSorley, Edward. **OUR OWN KIND.** 1946

Moynihan, James H. **THE LIFE OF ARCHBISHOP JOHN IRELAND.** 1953

Niehaus, Earl F. **THE IRISH IN NEW ORLEANS, 1800-1860.** 1965

O'Grady, Joseph Patrick. **IRISH-AMERICANS AND ANGLO-AMERICAN RELATIONS, 1880-1888.** 1976

Rodechko, James Paul. **PATRICK FORD AND HIS SEARCH FOR AMERICA:** A Case Study of Irish-American Journalism, 1870-1913. 1976

Roney, Frank. **IRISH REBEL AND CALIFORNIA LABOR LEADER:** An Autobiography. Edited by Ira B. Cross. 1931

Roohan, James Edmund. **AMERICAN CATHOLICS AND THE SOCIAL QUESTION, 1865-1900.** 1976

Shannon, James. **CATHOLIC COLONIZATION ON THE WESTERN FRONTIER.** 1957

Shaw, Douglas V. **THE MAKING OF AN IMMIGRANT CITY:** Ethnic and Cultural Conflict in Jersey City, New Jersey, 1850-1877. 1976

Sylvester, Harry. **MOON GAFFNEY.** 1947

Tarpey, Marie Veronica. **THE ROLE OF JOSEPH McGARRITY IN THE STRUGGLE FOR IRISH INDEPENDENCE.** 1976

Vinyard, JoEllen McNergney. **THE IRISH ON THE URBAN FRONTIER:** Nineteenth Century Detroit. 1976

Walsh, James P., ed. **THE IRISH: AMERICA'S POLITICAL CLASS.** 1976

Weisz, Howard Ralph. **IRISH-AMERICAN AND ITALIAN-AMERICAN EDUCATIONAL VIEWS AND ACTIVITIES, 1870-1900:** A Comparison. 1976